# FAKE
# NEWS

How Propaganda Influenced the 2016 Election,
A Historical Comparison to 1930's Germany

# FAKE
# NEWS

How Propaganda Influenced the 2016 Election,
A Historical Comparison to 1930's Germany

KELLY CAREY

MARZENHALE
PUBLISHING

Snow Hill, Maryland

ISBN 978-0-9986800-0-2

Library of Congress Control Number: 2017901659

Published in the United States of America by Marzenhale Publishing in Snow Hill, Maryland

www.marzenhalepublishing.com

10 9 8 7 6 5 4 3 2 1

PRINTED IN THE UNITED STATES OF AMERICA

*Dedicated to my parents.*

## ACKNOWLEDGEMENTS

I am grateful to Jean for her unending patience and guidance as this effort was underway, to Kim for making it seem like my grammar is much better than it is, and Aubree, for her patience and creativity.

PROPAGANDA: Ideas or statements, often false or exaggerated, spread in order to help a cause, a political leader, or a government.

*"Propaganda tries to force a doctrine on the whole people....* *Propaganda works on the general public from the standpoint of an* *idea and makes them ripe for the victory of this idea."* - Adolf Hitler, *Mein Kampf,* 1926.

# CONTENTS

# Introduction

It is widely accepted that propaganda played an enormous role in Adolf Hitler's coming to power in Germany in 1933.

For example, most people believe that Hitler was elected to be the leader, or *Führer*, of Germany. This is not the case. Although Germany was a democracy, on January 30, 1933, Hitler was *appointed* chancellor by President Paul Von Hindenburg under pressure from fellow conservatives and the National Socialist German Workers' Party — the Nazis. Hindenburg had been duly elected president in 1925 and re-elected in 1932, but was considered old and senile, and was losing popularity as quickly as Hitler was gaining it. Hindenburg died in 1934, but not before Hitler had the cabinet pass the "Law Concerning the Highest State Office of the Reich," which stipulated that upon Hindenburg's death, the offices of president and chancellor would be merged under the title of Leader and Chancellor (*Führer und Reichskanzler*). After Hindenburg's death, Adolf Hitler held a plebiscite election and won with 90 percent of the vote, though it didn't matter because he had already seized the reins of power. Fears of communism, a Jewish takeover, and the penalty of death for insurrection had already ripped through Germany. Hitler, as Chancellor and President was, effectively, a dictator. As they say, the rest is history.

I propose that propaganda also played a huge role in the 2016 American presidential election of Donald Trump. The theory presented is that it started with Fox News in 1996, ballooned in 2001 after the World Trade Center bombings, and culminated in the election of Donald Trump, a man who says he is superior because of his genes, and believes the country needs to rid itself of an entire religion. Sound familiar? If one has studied the Third Reich even a little, these facts should raise huge red flags about naming Trump the leader of the free world. For some reason, it does not draw even a raised eyebrow from many of our friends on the right. Most dismiss him as a fiery rabble rouser, likely to be reeled in by the seriousness of the office he will soon hold. In 1923, an American reporter named Hubert Knickerbocker said this of the rising leader in Germany: "The first impression he makes on any non-German is that he looks silly. I broke out laughing. He looks like a caricature of himself … he is softly fat about his hips and this gives his figure a curiously female appearance." (Nagorski, 40) Adolf Hitler was not so funny 10 years later.

There is a saying that those who do not know history are doomed to repeat it. In the 1920s and 1930s, the Germans managed to overlook the rise of the German National Socialist German Workers' Party, even though their motives were clear. Their ideology was laid out in the National Socialist Programme (also called the 25-point Programme or the 25-point Plan) in the 1920s that included not allowing Jews to be citizens. The plan included allowing only true blooded, Aryan Germans citizenship (members of "the race") posts in government and the benefits of society.

Everyone else was to be eradicated from Germany so the superior race could continue and thrive without being held back by Jews, homosexuals, the disabled, non-Germans, and other inferiors. If we trade 2016 Muslims/Mexicans for 1934 Jews and we trade German nationalism for American nationalism, are we not on the same track? In America, we have overlooked the rise of a far right ideology known as the "alt-right," which is just a disguised term for Neo-Nazi. This is a group who are white supremacists that believe whites are being defeated by loss of bloodlines through inter-breeding, immigration, religion, and any other manner of things they believe are being taken from them. The alt-right are afraid and they are empowered by Trump, who does not seem to mind getting votes from Nazis, as long as they put him in power. After Trump's election on November 8, 2016, there were over 900 instances of swastikas and various hate crimes from the Neo-Nazis throughout the United States.

You might say, "that can't happen here; we have checks and balances on power." So did Germany. Hitler and the Nazi Party eliminated their checks and balances by falsely blaming the Reichstag fire on Communists. In doing so, that allowed the Nazi Party to suspend the freedoms of regular citizens in order to save the German nation. Adolf Hitler and his party then controlled all the press. They suspended the right to assembly. They usurped free speech. Is it impossible to believe that the fervor and loyalists of the alt-right would not use a similar tactic to gain control now?

After the attacks on American soil on September 11, 2001, Congress willingly gave the powers of war to the sitting president, George W. Bush, who took us into a misguided, impossible war in Iraq and Afghanistan that was devoid of connection to the actual attacks of September 11. It is woefully short sighted to believe that the hatred of Muslims being fed to our friends on the right by "news" sources would lead to a rational, thoughtful approach in any kind of attack. The rhetoric demands elimination. Period.

It is my opinion that we have never seen a closer parallel in American history to the one that compares and contrasts the two volatile, persuasive propaganda machines of Germany in the two decades of 1920's and 1930's and the two decades of extreme right-wing American propaganda from 1996 to present. One would be an irresponsible student of history to not draw the parallels and encourage corrective measures as to avoid repeating one of the worst travesties known to man, The Holocaust. As students of History and Politics, we have the responsibility to properly research, document, and disseminate our findings, especially in the face of the dim future our country is now facing based on lies from the right.

Hitler rose to power in front of the world and created concentration camps to eliminate Jews in front of his German compatriots. He used lies and preconceived prejudices to fuel his fire. Hitler's rise was based on the principle that Aryan Germans were being eliminated by mixing bloodlines, and "the race" would soon be eliminated. Ann Coulter, a popular right-wing pundit bases her hatred of Mexicans on the same idea – they are coming for the sole purpose of eliminating Caucasians. She said that. Out loud.

Adolf Hitler named Josef Goebbels to head the Public Enlightenment and Propaganda wing of the Nazi Party. He joined the Nazi party in 1924 and had been a loyal member, serving on one of the Nazi newspapers. He was attracted to the party by Hitler's commitment and fiery speeches. Goebbels' was also a gifted speaker, and used his oratory skills to further the Nazi movement as well. An educated man, Goebbels earned his doctorate in German Philology from the University of Hindenburg. He was born with a birth defect that kept him from joining the military and made him feel inferior. His job within the Nazi party was to make it not only palatable to the public but positive and desirable. He had to lie about political opponents, ignore his own party's shortcomings, and lessen the blow of some of the more radical policies. His job was to make Nazis seem nice. In 1933 after Hitler was named Chancellor, Goebbels wrote, "Now it will be easy, for we can call on the resources of the State. Radio and press at our disposal. We shall stage a masterpiece of propaganda." (Farquhar, 96) Of course, he fulfilled that promise with one of the greatest propaganda machines ever developed.

In June 2016, Donald Trump hired his "Goebbels," a man named Steven Bannon. He is an anti-Semite, white supremacist who runs a Neo-Nazi propaganda Web site called the Breitbart News Network (Breitbart). He took over day-to-day activities at Breitbart in 2012 after Andrew Breitbart passed away suddenly. Mr. Breitbart billed Breitbart.com as an alternative news site along the same lines as propaganda website The Drudge Report, run by Breitbart's hero Matt Drudge. Like Goebbels, Bannon is an educated man having earned two masters' degrees, one from Georgetown University and one from Harvard University, after earning his bachelor's degree from Virginia Tech. People on the right defend Bannon when he is criticized for being a white supremacist with the argument that he is educated. Of course, one does not nullify the other, but it seems to be their excuse. In some circles one cannot be racist and have a degree from Georgetown University. No one tell the late Antonin Scalia. I think these smaller nuances that link the American "news" and the propaganda that brought Hitler to power in the 1930's cannot be ignored. Instead, they are the most important pieces; they are the hints of Nazi Germany similarities that should jar us into the reality of who exactly the next leader of the free world is.

A brief introduction of the Tea Party and the Freedom Caucus is in order before we delve into the details of propaganda in the 2016 election cycle in comparison to Hitler's propaganda. The Tea Party was a grassroots movement that started in 2009 to oppose President Barack Obama's plan to help homeowners caught in the middle of the housing bubble. It was started by a group of people that called themselves "constitutionalists" and who built a movement around the idea of small government, personal responsibility, lower taxes, and reducing the national debt. Most of their factions avoided public positions on social issues such as same-sex marriage or abortion. Members of the Tea Party tried to stay focused on small government and lower taxes. For the most part, Republicans have stepped away from the strict, uncompromising views that halt progress; however, there are still Tea Party members and a movement of sorts.

The Freedom Caucus was started in 2015. It is a Congressional caucus in the House of Representatives that represents right-wing views and is believed to be an extension of the Tea Party. This group was found to be difficult to deal with within the House, and John Boehner, then Speaker of the House, was not offering Freedom Caucus members leadership positions, causing a rebellion. They began to block all of the Speaker's bills and dead locked the Republican Party that was actually in power. Boehner eventually resigned his speakership at the behest of the Freedom Caucus and, soon after, Paul Ryan was elected as Speaker of the House. Due to the difficulties faced by Boehner, Ryan insisted on having the blessing of the Freedom Caucus so he would not appear to have a deadlocked House, considering him a powerless Speaker. The Freedom Caucus are a small group of Republicans, but have showed tenacity and the ability to stall progress and get their way more often than not.

Detailed exploration into the Tea Party and the Freedom Caucus and the ultimate effect of these two groups on the GOP is a book in and of itself. This effort on propaganda will not sacrifice space and time for their full explanation. But some of the players later may be referred to as Tea Party sympathizers or a member of the Freedom Caucus. Interestingly, Adolf Hitler was also attracted to a small, extreme faction of the right wing party after World War I. Called the German Worker's Party and later known as later the National Socialist German Worker's Party or Nazi Party, Hitler was a visitor at their meetings as a spy for the army that was seeking and eliminating Marxists. What he found was a group of people that shared his nationalistic and economic views. In this political upheaval and stark divisions of the right wing political party in 1920's Germany, Hitler found a place to rise up and be a leader. One would be remiss not to draw the parallel that saw Donald Trump rise out of a broken GOP with a new Speaker and the noticeable division between the old guard Republicans and new guard – the Tea Party/Constitutionalists.

*In a hundred years' time, perhaps, a great man will appear who may offer them (the Germans) a chance at salvation. He'll take me as a model, use my ideas, and follow the course I have charted.*—Adolf Hitler

Chapter 1

*If you tell a big enough lie and tell it frequently, it will be believed.* – Adolf Hitler

But how? How can the most evil, primitive, and vile ideas become popular? Why did educated, seemingly average people think genocide a good idea? Adolf Hitler was promoted on a clear platform of discrimination, hate, and fear. For one, he was popular. People honestly believed he was the only hope to preserve Germany and therefore, Germans. There was no question in the minds of the Germans that Adolf Hitler would bring Germany and Germans wealth and pride. The question remained, though – how did he do it? Why was the elimination of Jews, homosexuals, disabled persons, and non-Germans ok?

There are many answers to the question we all ask when we think about the Holocaust. One rightly wonders how a man could gain the confidence of the populace when his idea is so harmful and awful to an entire group of people. Anti-Semitism was not relegated to Germany at the turn of the $20^{th}$ century. Rather, it could be considered a cancer that continued to spread throughout Europe, the Far East and the Americas. Karl Marx feared the economic strength of Jews and began to think of them not as a religion, an ethnicity, or a culture, but an economic and social powerhouse transcending national boundaries. (Hamerow, 19) After World War I, Jews seemed to be the only group in Europe that was flourishing and were proud that they were now equal to their brethren. Some Jews also sensed the growing hostility towards their people and found solace in the Communist Party, further alienating them from their fellow Europeans. (28) Many blamed Jews for the Great Depression in 1929, in which the world saw Jews seemingly not suffer as much as the rest of the world. Some even thought Jewish bankers orchestrated the crash to fill their coffers at the expense of Christians and others. Many thought democracy had found a permanent home in European countries in the 1920's after World War I. However, the 1929 market crash opened the door for authoritarian governments all over Europe, including Hungary, Poland, and the Baltic States. (34) What the world witnessed in the first 30 years of the 20th century, was Europe, having an inherent "problem" with their Jewish population. The Europeans, especially Germans, were suffering from economic and social despair following the World War. Equally jarring, they developed a very convenient scapegoat for all their problems – the Jews.

It's clear from day one of Hitler's meteoric rise in the 1920's that propaganda played a huge role. In his book, Mein Kampf, Hitler claims to have learned the value of propaganda as a soldier in the First World War. He expressed an understanding of how effective British propaganda gave the Brits an upper hand in the war, and how the ineffective German propaganda demoralized the German troops. Hitler described effective propaganda as being not too intellectual, for it must appeal to the least intellectual of its intended audience. The propaganda must also appeal to feelings, not intellect, and it must tug at the heart strings of many. He thought that because most people were not intelligent they waver from one idea to the next, and therefore they were pliable as long as one was tugging at their sentimentalities. He also stated effective propaganda gave only one side of the story, never giving any positive notions to the enemy because masses have feeble minds and could not force themselves to think of any other positives. The Nazi party in its infant stages in the 1920's had little access to any media and relied on Hitler's speeches to spread their massage. This gave rise to the notion that supporting the Nazi's extreme anti-Semitism was not a minority opinion and that they had a voice. These feelings they had for decades about the rise of the Jews and the "fall" of their own Aryan bloodlines were true and justified, and they had found a leader to help their cause of saving themselves.

Muslims have also been attacked viciously by the right wing media, even before the September 11, 2001, terrorist attacks. It has been suggested that the Muslims are a threat to Christianity worldwide. They have been vilified and questioned since the Founders wrote the Constitution. Some of the Founding Fathers were preferential to a "religious test" before becoming President or otherwise holding office in the United States. They thought a Muslim should not be allowed to serve in or for our government. Unfortunately, little has changed in regards to that sentiment. Muslims have always been a shadow society, having different religious beliefs, different attire, and a different language. In short – Muslims simply worship differently than Anglo Saxon America is used to seeing people worship. We fear what we do not understand; and the conservative right is driving their point home by the spreading of misinformation. The reports from conservative media are that all Muslims are evil terrorists; that Muslims are trying to take over the world and banish Christianity from the earth. Do not get me wrong, some are. There are terrorists that believe they are serving Allah by ridding the earth of Christians. There are also Christians that want to rid the world of Muslims. Glenn Beck wrote a book in 2015 titled It IS About Islam. It is a pseudo-intellectual attempt to completely condemn Islam without completely condemning Islamists. What? Did I make a typo? No. Unfortunately, the book is an attempt to vilify an entire religion without vilifying an entire religion. Beck writes about Islamic splits and how awful they are worldwide. He laments that even in their differences they find solid ground in an apocalyptic end for the world via Muslim extremism. Beck finishes the book like a true conservative - imploring his readers to "take their country back" and to "not lose sight of God." It is important to remember that this is the same guy who thinks the Israelis have a right to that little strip of land called the Gaza Strip where they are in a constant battle against the Palestinians for occupancy because in "the end times," according to biblical prophecy, Israelis must live there for Jesus Christ to return and - yes, you guessed it - end the world.

Yes, the seed for Islamophobia was planted long ago, and when the attacks occurred on September 11th, most knew it would not be easy to be Muslim in America. Fox "News" started the rhetoric 5 years prior to the September 11th attacks, and found a listening audience. Fox "News" was founded because Rupert Murdoch and Roger Ailes felt their conservative voices were not being heard. No one was reporting the (supposed) immediate threat of Muslims and Mexicans and the thinning of our Anglo Saxon bloodlines! Never mind the outright assault on Christianity. Remember - Hitler stated that propaganda was not be too intellectual. Fox "News" took heed and attacked what everyone knows a little bit about but most do not know a lot about – Christmas. People were trying to be too politically correct and too nice, and this was a direct attempt to crucify them as Christians because they could not say "Merry Christmas." Now, keep in mind, one has always been able to say "Merry Christmas." There were instances of businesses, in an attempt to be inclusive and not make people that did not celebrate Christmas feel uncomfortable, saying things like "Happy Holidays" rather than "Merry Christmas.". It is also okay to curse on your own time, but cursing is not ok when handing someone their hamburger. Employers have always reserved the right to be inclusive (or not) and screen what their employees say while earning their paycheck. There are a lot of things one cannot do as a representative of their company that are just fine to do on their own time. But somehow and in some way Fox "News" has viewers believing that this "assault" on Christmas is a step away from being beheaded - right here in America! It is such a long leap, yet it is believed. The right wing pundits – Fox "News", Glenn Beck, Rush Limbaugh, Sean Hannity, and others - feed off this fear that brown people are taking your things – your bloodlines, your jobs, your wives, your water, your religion. Everything. Gone. Much like the Germans were told the Jews were doing to them in the first few decades of the 20th century.

Adolf Hitler was attempting to take over the government of Germany in 1933. He was already Chancellor, but he needed all the powers of the police and press to pull off what he hoping to accomplish – world domination and the annihilation of all Jews. The communists still held enough power and influence to be a problem, and Hitler needed a solution. Nazis set fire to The Reichstag Building, Germany's parliament, on February 27, 1933, just days before the election on March 5. It was a desperate move, but Hitler was a desperate man running out of time. He immediately blamed the fire on Communist leadership and was able to get the backing of the government to suspend the rights of press, speech, and assembly for the safety of the German people. Hitler's propaganda machine was in full swing and the people believed that Communists were going to win the elections and that the Soviets would soon take over Germany. Hitler's Nazis now controlled information. His voice was to ring over the radio airwaves for the next 12 years, disparaging Communists and Jews, and praising pure-blooded Germans. Hitler won the election, but not by a majority. He garnered 44 percent of the vote, and combining the seats of Nazi party and the Nationalist party in the parliament, Hitler had a majority. Within weeks the German Constitution was just a remnant of what it had been. Germany went from a democracy to a dictatorship while all of Germany and the world watched in amazement. (Hoyt, 31)

Polls taken of Americans in February 1941 showed that Americans found Jews to be more of a threat than Germans - 18% to 14%. That number slipped in 1942 to 15 percent feeling the Jews were a threat to 18 percent for Germans. That was the only year

Germans were found to be more threatening than Jews. Remarkable. The United States was going to war with Germany, yet the Jews were the threat worldwide to lifestyles and finances. (Hamerow, XV) Part of the problem was the fact that being an anti-Semite at the turn of the $20^{th}$ century was par for the course, not only in Germany, but around the world. Many people thought the Jews had too much power and were controlling world finance. One of the reasons anti-Semitism was ignored in Germany was because it was prevalent in almost all the political parties. Everyone had an opinion about "solving" the "Jewish problem." (Goldhagen, 84) Fast forward to 2016 Donald Trump's exact words when calling for the ban of Muslims were, "Donald J. Trump is calling for a total and complete shutdown of Muslims entering the United States until our country's representatives can figure out what is going on." That corresponds with a Muslim "problem" that needs to be solved. According to a Pew Research Center poll conducted in 2015, 55 percent of Americans have an unfavorable view of Muslims. Clearly, there is plenty of support for solving the "Muslim problem" here in America, much like Hitler solved the "Jewish problem" in Germany in the 1930's and 1940's.

The Neo-Nazi movement in America had its own "Reichstag Fire" moment following the attacks on September 11, 2001. Neo-Nazi's had always been around, hoping for their moment to shine and be a political force in the United States. And they began peeking through the cracks of right wing "news," and the fear machine was in full swing right after the attacks on September 11, 2001. Playing on the fear of the moment, on September 12, 2001, Ann Coulter stated, "We know who the homicidal maniacs are. They are the ones cheering and dancing right now. We should invade their countries, kill their leaders, and convert them to Christianity." So, for Coulter, the answer to extreme religious fanaticism is extreme religious fanaticism? Kill Muslims in the name of Jesus Christ? I am sure He would be proud. But the right finally had their Reichstag, and they were going full steam ahead with their propaganda machine, even if it was intellectually inane. In 2003 Coulter said, "I just can't imagine anyone not seeing 9/11 as a really good reason for wiping out Islamic totalitarians."

What is an Islamic totalitarian? Is it a leader from an Islamic country? Is it any Muslim that pushes extreme beliefs? Is it someone that wants everyone to be Muslim? By making such a loaded statement without clarifying what an Islamic totalitarian is, Coulter fires up her followers and allows them to draw their own conclusions. And remember, people that believe propaganda do not do any research because the propaganda appears to have all the answers.

Fred Vultee, a PhD. from the University of Missouri researched a phenomenon known as Orientalism in regard to the Fox "News" coverage of Islam. He concluded that the coverage provided by Fox "News" was painted Islam in a particularly negative light and was used to promote an endless war against an invisible enemy. He stated:

A visit any day to the Web site of the Fox News Channel is likely to offer yet another piece of a sinister puzzle: the looming threat of Islam to everything the West holds dear. There is an armed threat, of course, in Afghanistan and Iraq and possibly as near as the shopping mall. But there is also a cultural danger that menaces all of Europe, that stalks coffee shops and classrooms, that endangers individual children and entire health-care systems with its irreducible demands, that hates Barbie and Valentine's Day and even the Three Little Pigs. And even as the West watches, *they* have overtaken *us* as the world's largest religion.

That is pretty scary rhetoric. Certainly, at a minimum, this is "news" with the purpose of guiding one's thoughts on Islam. And it seems Neo-Nazi republicans were waiting in the wings for such words to take over the right and strike fear into the hearts of anyone watching and hoping they would not actually look anything up.

Steve Bannon has always had the goal of taking over the Republican Party to further his racist agenda. In 2013 Bannon lamented the lack of a true Conservative party in the United States when he stated, "It's going to be an insurgent, center-right populist movement that is virulently anti-establishment, and it's going to continue to hammer this city." Bannon's agenda has been no secret and when he was named to Donald Trump's campaign team, the Neo-Nazi's in America gave a collective high five to Trump for making their ignorant positions main stream again. David Duke, former grand master of the KKK, said the Bannon choice was "Excellent, and basically creating the ideological aspects of where we're going." Peter Brimelow of the racist Web site Vdare, Jared Taylor of racist American Renaissance, and Broad Griffen of Occidental Dissent praise Trump's hire of Bannon by calling it "amazing."

Bannon's Web site has been "welcome home to some of the most outspoken Neo-Nazis of our time, such as Pamela Geller and Robert Spencer. Geller is a known Islamophobe and Spencer is considered the leader of Neo-Nazis in America today. Together they started the American Freedom Defense Initiative, a group that has been designated a hate group by the Anti-Defamation League and the Southern Poverty Law Center. Neither Spencer nor Geller is allowed to travel to the United Kingdom because of their vicious rhetoric. *The New York Times* joined in on the propaganda by not saying exactly what Bannon is, a Neo-Nazi. The newspaper published a profile on Bannon, casting him as a "combative populist." Buried deep within the profile is an account of Bannon talking about his belief in the "genetic superiority" of certain people and his support for restricting voting rights to only property owners. Adolf Hitler had believed in the genetic superiority of pure-blooded Germans since 1912. Bannon is fully aware he is leading a movement of hate. In an interview with *MotherJones*, he stated:

"Are there racist people involved in the alt-right? Absolutely. Look, are there some people that are white nationalists that are attracted to some of the philosophies of the alt-right? Maybe. Are there some people that are anti-Semitic that are attracted? Maybe. Right? Maybe some people are attracted to the alt-right that are homophobes, right? But that's just like, there are certain elements of the progressive left and the hard left that attract certain elements."

Bannon's Web site, Breitbart.com, has been less than covert when letting its Nazi flag fly.

Linking to a "flashback" story about (George) Soros' financial role supporting "legal battles against state voting laws," the Breitbart Twitter account tweeted on November 28, 2016, "Like an octopus." The "octopus" wording is overt anti-Semitic rhetoric dating back to at least the 1930's, when it was a common theme in Nazi propaganda. The imagery of a Jewish octopus engulfing the globe or ensnaring political institutions can be found on other white supremacist and Neo-Nazi online forums, as well as on Fox News' airwaves. Bill O'Reilly, a Fox "News" host, also used overtly anti-Semitic imagery by referring to George Soros, a liberal philanthropist responsible for such things as Open Society and Center for American Progress. This seems innocuous, a right wing pundit taking jabs at a philanthropist for progressive think tanks like Center for American Progress and OpenSource. No big deal right? A quick Google search of George Soros leads a studious reader to his Jewish history. In Austria. In the 1940's. A man whose father's last name was Schwartz, but had to be changed to protect his family from the Nazis who were occupying Hungary. This is a man who had a sense for markets almost unmatched in the twentieth century, was able to speculate on currency and then give billions away for democracies worldwide. Soros said this about his successes, "This allows me to take a stand on controversial issues: In fact, it obliges me to do so because others cannot." This is the man that the right has chosen to demonize with anti-Semitic undertones.

Bannon and Trump. Goebbels and Hitler. We have seen this show before, and we know how it ends. Just as Hitler wanted to rid the world of Jews and further the superior genes of Aryan Germans, so does Bannon. And, by definition then, so does Trump, because he picked the Neo-Nazi to be in his administration and follows his direction. Trump seems to listen to whoever spoke to him last or, quite possibly, no one at all. He claims to have "a really good brain" and just watches TV to get his international news. At any rate, Trump is satisfied to tout Nazi ideas and wishes to ban an entire religion or tattoo them, or otherwise "keep track and monitor" them. The parallels between the Trump propaganda machine and the Hitler propaganda machine are overwhelming when it comes to the ideology of the people closest to them. Both Trump and Bannon and Hitler and Goebbels blamed their enemies – Muslims and Jews, respectively – for offenses that were not their making. They also used the media to help disseminate their fake "news" stories. And, just like in the 1920's, no one seems to have noticed.

## Chapter 2

*An 'extremely credible source' has called my office and told me that Barack Obama's birth certificate is a fraud*—Donald Trump

Donald Trump was promoted on a clear platform of discrimination, hate, and fear. He was popular. People honestly believed he was the only hope to preserve the United States of America and, therefore, Americans. There was no question in the minds of those on the conservative right that Trump would bring America and Americans wealth and pride. Again, we ask how? How can a man with no grasp of civics, no grasp of the parameters of the job for which he is applying, and no applicable experience gain the confidence and the vote of 60 million people?

Propaganda! The name "low information voter" came about in the early 1990's in a book by Samuel Popkin titled <u>The Reasoning Voter: Communication and Persuasion in Presidential Elections</u>. Popkin's book concludes that voters make their decisions less on factual issues and more on feelings and the popularity of the candidate.

One of the first things Donald Trump said after announcing his candidacy for the Republican nomination for President of the United States was that he was going to build a wall on our southern border, between Mexico and the United States, and have Mexico pay for it. Silly, right? Most of us on the left laughed at such a proposition. Having a general idea of how sovereign nations work, we know the President of the United States does not get to make such decisions for the Mexican government. You know who didn't laugh? The people watching Fox News and reading Breitbart.com. They had been spoon fed immigrant horror stories for years. If one watched either of these outlets, you believed tens of thousands of people were marching over the border monthly, weekly, possibly even daily, and murdering one for every three Americans they met! And the ball was rolling.

Just as Hitler began his assault on the non-Germans, particularly Jews, the disabled, and homosexuals, the right began their assault on our southern border decades prior. Ronald Reagan's policy on immigration is much different than the current conservative policy. He signed into law the Immigration Reform and Control Act of 1986. The legislation made the employer responsible for their employees' immigration status, allowed for seasonal agricultural workers, made it illegal to knowingly hire illegal aliens, and, most controversially, allowed illegal aliens who had been in the country for a certain amount of time pay a fine and be on the track to citizenship. This amnesty will get you on the fast track out of the Conservative party nowadays. It is difficult to find a conservative who would be willing to admit that their hero, Ronald Reagan, was seeking amnesty for illegal aliens.

Then came the propaganda. In the 1990's Bill Clinton had to satisfy our friends and brothers in Mexico and further abroad that as a country we would not consider mass deportations. Republicans were calling for the removal of all illegal aliens immediately – and by force. (Clinton, 2004, 756) was fairly strict about enforcing the immigration laws of our country, deporting 30,000 illegal aliens from 1993 to 1996. (Clinton, 1996, 134) However, the facts already did not matter. The right was assaulting policies that had been pushed by both parties for decades as one sided. The right wing pundits said that these amnesty policies were being advanced in order to secure the vote of immigrant Mexicans for Democrats. As is usually the case, there is a catch to the right wing propaganda machine. And the catch here? Undocumented immigrants do not vote. There is no evidence of that. It is a false narrative designed to vilify the left and demonize our Mexican friends south of the border. It is propaganda because it used falsified information to push a narrative for a political group. The other notion is that the Mexicans earn citizenship and, after gaining amnesty and citizenship, they vote republican because republican ideas are so good for the working class. When the choices are "democrats are doing things to get illegal votes" or "we need Mexicans to vote for our great policies" as a republican, one must go for the first option, even if it is really stupid.

The advent of Fox News changed "news" forever. The ultimate propaganda "news" organization hires only conservative hosts. In the beginning, it was required. Bill O'Reilly admits readily that the slogan "We report, you decide" would be more accurate if it stated "We report, we decide." So much for objectively reporting news. Roger Ailes, the brains behind the Fox News propaganda machine stated in 1995, "One of the problems we have to work on here together when we start this network is that most journalists are liberals. And we've got to fight that." Reporters and staffers knew from the outset that Fox, despite its insistence on being "fair and balanced," was going to present news with a conservative slant, and if that did not suit them, they would not be at Fox long. So it began, no more just reporting what is happening, the propaganda machine began reporting as they needed the news to be to push their own agenda – also known as propaganda.

As the right became more vocal about Mexicans coming across the border, the vitriol from the pundit class became more and more extreme. Ann Coulter has been particularly vile when discussing our friends south of the border. She is so popular amongst the right, it seems President-Elect Trump used her immigration plan to attract voters already versed in the hatred of the right. On the Bill O'Reilly show on April 13, 2006, she stated, "I'd build a wall. In fact, I'd hire illegal immigrants to build the wall. And throw out all the illegals who are here. … It's cheap labor." Ann Coulter is a Tea Party darling, and is a sought after pundit and an "authority" on Fox "News". At the time this book was written, Coulter was frequently interviewed by propaganda organizations, was a syndicated columnist, and appeared on numerous radio programs.

Coulter continued her assault on "illegal immigration," and in 2007 she lamented the fact that in 1960 whites made up 90% of the population and now whites account for only about 65% of the population. She actually calls this genocide. She stated that she feared this new majority would not be as compassionate as white leadership has been in America. (Slavery? Women voting? African Americans voting? "Colored" water fountains? She has an odd view of compassion.) She claimed that the current immigration law was designed to reduce white peoples' percentage in the population. The problem with all of this is that it is patently false. No one has ever stated that their goals for allowing immigrants, legal or illegal, to enter the U.S. were to water down the bloodline of American Caucasians. It's scary rhetoric that makes people fear they are losing their place in society. And it works. I have heard many friends on the right claim the Mexicans are taking our jobs, things, wives, lifestyle, etc., etc.

One of the more consistent anomalies in right-wing propaganda is that there is often some shred of truth. There is no doubt that whites were 90% of population and are now 65%. That seems reasonable. It is the enormous, irresponsible, and false statement that our immigration policies are set *for the purpose of reducing white people's place in society.* There is simply no evidence to support that assertion. It is false. And false news is propaganda. She is demonizing a group of people to achieve a certain ideal. She has a large audience that thinks she is an expert and they are full of fear and she is one of the people creating and guiding scare tactics that make humans believe lies. She makes a true statement and then connects it to some obscure dot not even in sight of the truth, and low information voters think she's a genius.

Another quote from Coulter from 2015: "If you don't want to be killed by ISIS, don't go to Syria, if you don't want to be killed by a Mexican, there's nothing I can tell you." She also said, "Illegal immigrants are not only at our doorstep, but millions of them are already through the door, murdering more Americans than ISIS ever will." Sigh. Patently false. Propaganda. A report by the American Immigration Council states:

*"Immigrants are less likely to commit serious crimes or be behind bars than the native-born, and high rates of immigration are associated with lower rates of violent crime and property crime. This holds true for both legal immigrants and the unauthorized, regardless of their country of origin or level of education. In other words, the overwhelming majority of immigrants are not "criminals" by any commonly accepted definition of the term."*

Again, there are millions here. That is a true statement. It is the conclusion that Coulter draws to push her narrative that the "brown" people are taking our things, including our history and bloodlines. Her assertion that Mexicans are running around murdering Americans for sport is simply false. And very dangerous. And, for some reason, people believe her.

Adolf Hitler said similar things about groups of people he detested and wanted to eliminate to promote German Nationalism. He was adamant that others were trying to water down the gifted, strong Aryan bloodline. The Nazis believed Germans were superior to Jews and other groups including gypsies, the disabled, homosexuals, and Afro-Germans. He felt the only way to hurt the German race was to mix races and cause the superior genes to degenerate. The Nazis believed the only solution was to eradicate the Jews, which they looked at as a race, not a religion. "Exploiting pre-existing images and stereotypes, Nazi propagandists portrayed Jews as an "alien race" that fed off the host nation, poisoned its culture, seized its economy, and enslaved its workers and farmers." Sound familiar? It should, on his own conservative radio show April 1, 2005, Rush Limbaugh said, "So invasive species like mollusks and spermatozoa are not good, and we've got a federal judge say, "You can't bring it in here," but invasive species in the form of illegal immigration is fine and dandy."

By dehumanizing Mexicans, the right-wing pundits make it easier for their followers to treat them as less than people. Animals. Aliens. Adolf Hitler accomplished this by referring to non-Germans, especially Jews, as aliens. Rush Limbaugh stated, "Isn't protecting our legal citizens from an invading army of illegal aliens who are using our services and taking our jobs, isn't that a basic notion of fairness?" (His radio show, April 26, 2010) An invading army? From 2010 to 2011 we saw a drop in illegal immigrants in the United States from 11,600,000 to 11,500,000. (http://immigration.procon.org/view.resource.php?resourceID=0008 44) Hardly an army coming across the border. But the people that listen(ed) to Rush Limbaugh, and Ann Coulter, and Adolf Hitler, do/did not look things up. It is simply believed. What the pundits are saying fits their narrative of white fragility and the perceived fear that the "brown" people are taking their stuff.

Coulter stated, "Israel says, quite correctly, that changing Israel's ethnicity would change Israel. Well, changing America's ethnicity changes the idea of America, too." It is clear that Israel's ethnicity is historically important to some AND is based in thousands of years of history and has to do with prophecy in the Bible and keeping the "one true church" intact. In fact, strict Zionists believe that Jesus Christ cannot return unless true Jews are living in the Holy Land. What is America's ethnicity? Did anyone ask Coulter? Is it English? Irish? Catholic? Native American? Mormon? Exactly which ethnicity are we preserving? She also stated, "Democrats denounce and abuse white people." So, maybe to Coulter, white is an ethnicity comparable to Judaism? Her argument relies on the false premise that America has an inherit ethnicity comparable to the ethnicity the Israeli's claim. We do not. We are less than 300 years old. Coulter may be wishing to go back to when only free white males could vote and African Americans counted for 3/5ths of a man. Let us hope not.

Right wing propaganda managed to demonize Mexicans to the point that some Americans think it is a good idea to spend upwards of $28 billion to build a wall. Of course, Trump says he will have Mexico pay for it. There comes a time, after listening to Trump, that thinking citizens just stare back and wait for him to realize what he just said. It is then that you realize he was serious. Estimates to deport 11 million undocumented immigrants would cost anywhere from $285 million to $600 million and take 20 years. And there are people on the right that believe the rhetoric and are literally scared for their lives that want this to be the first thing President-Elect Trump does. Unfortunately, they have again been fed bad information. At least 40 percent, and most researchers estimate the number to actually be closer to 50 percent, of foreigners in this country arrive here illegally by airplane. They arrive legally on a commercial flight, with their work or student visa, and then overstay their welcome. So Trump and his followers are willing to spend almost $300 billion to stop half of the illegal immigrants from entering America. What about the other half? Are they not as dangerous? Are they not taking our jobs? Trump seems to think all illegal immigrants come from Mexico. It is really bizarre.

Of course, Donald Trump simply parrots what the right wing Neo-Nazis want to hear. He repeats lines from Fox "News", quotes Breitbart and retweets Nazis on Twitter, and his fans love it. One of Trump's more controversial lines this campaign season was in his speech to announce he was in fact running for the Republican nomination for President:

> "When Mexico sends its people, they're not sending their best. They're not sending you. They're not sending you. They're sending people that have lots of problems, and they're bringing those problems with us. They're bringing drugs. They're bringing crime. They're rapists. And some, I assume, are good people."

And on the left, we simply cringe that not only did our now President-Elect say that out loud, he said it in a speech for the whole world to hear. It is so embarrassing. Most studies find when Immigration, Customs, and Enforcement (ICE) releases prisoners that have yet to be tried for any offense or deported, less than 10 percent commit a criminal act and find themselves back in the hands of ICE. The *Boston Globe* did their own outlier study in a few surrounding states in their region and found the number to be closer to 30 percent. That is A LOT right? Well, no, it is not a lot. Among prisoners in state prisons in America, studies show that 67 percent return within three years and about 77 are arrested in five years. So, immigrant recidivism in prisons is about 12 percent of what our own is? These are the people being labeled criminals? The people who are less likely to commit repeat crimes than jailed Americans? If one watches only Fox "News" or reads only Breitbart, they do not know we are much more violent and prone to crime than our friends from south of the border. So Trump's narrative is not only harmful, it is completely false. More propaganda, so you can build that wall, Mr. Trump.

In Germany during the 1930's and 1940's, Jewish evil filled the conversation. It was all anyone in Germany talked about during that time period, and it was not positive accolades of people they had known their entire lives. They talked about Jews being the source of every ill that had befallen Germany, and any future threats could be attributed to the evil Jews as well. Of course, the results were predictable. Soon, Jews were being attacked and savagely beaten. Jewish-owned businesses were marked with the Star of David or the word "Jude" and gentiles entering the businesses were photographed. The pictures would then be made public for the purposes of humiliating and harassing them. Melita Maschmann writes in her memoir written to her lost childhood Jewish friend:

> *"Those* Jews were and remained something mysteriously menacing and anonymous. They were not the sum of all Jewish individuals... They were an evil power, something

with the attributes of a spook. One could not see it, but it was there, an active force of evil."

Maschmann goes on to describe the feelings towards Jews as so very evil and negative, yet no one could really pinpoint who these elusive Jews were. Also, Maschmann knew she could hate the Jews while still having individual relationships with certain Jews. Her parents were friendly with Jewish neighbors and colleagues, but talked about how awful they were when they were not around. Goldhagen states, "some of the central qualities of German Anti-Semitism: its hallucinatory image of the Jews; the specter of evil that they appeared to be casting over Germany." It became the collective consciousness of Germany. (Goldhagen, 88-9)

The vitriol on the right towards Mexicans is not much different than that of Jews in Nazi Germany. It is a specter. It is a hallucinogen. The right tries desperately to justify their hatred of Mexicans, but their reasons for hatred are easily debunked. Mexicans make up about half of our illegal population. And the right-wing pundits' craven appetite for revenge is insatiable. They get fired up when their dear leader, Trump, speaks ill of the enemy, and they cheer when they find a single Mexican in a sea of millions committing a crime. They told-you-so. It is those people who are terrible.

Kathryn Steinle was killed by the ricochet bullet of Francisco Sanchez, a man in the United States illegally and who had been deported and returned 5 times. He was a felon, wanted in Texas, and had been here illegally since 2009. He was an awful character and had no business being in this country in the position to steal a gun and murder someone. But he is one example out of 11 million illegal immigrants in the United States. And, as we learned before, 76 percent of all released felons find themselves back in prison after being released. Where is Trump's wall to keep those felons away from Americans? Do people really honestly believe they are going to be killed by Mexicans in America? Of course they do – because Ann Coulter told them to be afraid.

Until pundits on the right are willing to tell their loyal listeners the truth, or until their listeners learn to do the research to find the truth, Mexicans – illegal or not – will always be a punching bag. They are an easy target. They pay taxes and they want desperately to be here. A study in the *Wall Street Journal* stated 30 percent of Americans had a non-traffic offense by the age of 23. Most put the percent of criminals amongst illegal immigrants – only half of which are Mexicans – to be less than 10 percent. Republicans consistently refer to three families of people that suffered at the hands of illegal immigrants to push the narrative that they were simply criminals coming here to take advantage of unwitting Americans. This is, of course, patently untrue. From 1990 to 2013, undocumented immigrants in the United States tripled, yet their violent crime rate was cut in half during that time. Almost three percent of Mexican men age 18-39 in the U.S. For native-born men in the same age range, the incarceration rate is far higher, at 10 percent. Native-born men are three times more likely to be incarcerated. The right wing news simply is not telling their listeners and watchers the truth, much like Adolf Hitler and Josef Goebbels simply did not tell the truth about Jewish people and gained the support of Germans everywhere.

## Chapter 3

*How fortunate for governments that the people they administer don't think.* – Adolf Hitler

The reason Hitler was able to convince a nation that the destruction of an entire religion was necessary to preserve Germany is partly because he started long before 1934. His propaganda machine was in full force in 1920, when he listed the 25 points of the Nazis and the German Nationalist People's Party. He singled out Jews in point four "4. Only those who are our fellow countrymen can become citizens. Only those who have German blood, regardless of creed, can be our countrymen. Hence no Jew can be a countryman." Because of this, people who believed Germany itself, and therefore Germans, were being threatened by perceived non-Germans, Jews, homosexuals and others began to spread this rhetoric. They began repeating as if their very lives depended on it. Propaganda is a very powerful tool when one believes their rights or place in society is being threatened by people deemed less important than by a trusted leader.

"Donald J. Trump is calling for a total and complete shutdown of Muslims entering the United States until our country's representatives can figure out what is going on," a campaign press release said. Again, this assertion is laughable and easily dismissed to believers in the freedom of religion. Not so to our friends on the right who are susceptible to propaganda. How can they believe that banning an entire religion is a good idea in a country that was founded on freedom of religion? Literally. However, a quick perusal of some headlines of propaganda sites gathers the following information: 14 September 2015, Breitbart.com, A perplexing article bemoaning the influx of 1.5 million Muslims into the U.S., with "verified" stories of 6 being dangerous. A search of the Archives of The Drudge Report in 2009 with the keyword "Muslim" returns 1,019 entries; 1,019 negative or anti-Muslim entries about Muslims in a single year.

Adolf Hitler called for the total shut down of Jews upon becoming dictator in 1933. It is eerily familiar. Germany was the Weimar Republic from 1919 until 1933, when Adolf Hitler stole the leadership of the country. During this time, the murmurings of the "Jewish problem" were running rampant through Germany. Foreign journalists heard the murmurings, but did not see much proof that Jews were really in grave danger. Abraham Plotkin was a Jewish American labor organizer that arrived in Germany in 1932, hoping to study the labor movement. Upon meeting Jews in Berlin, they would ask if Jews were treated as poorly in America as they were in Germany. Plotkin stated that of course there was anti-Semitism in America, much like here. He did not notice anything that made him take notice of maleficence against Jews that was more alarming than anything he had seen in America. Plotkin was dubious that Hitler would actually seize power. He did not seem to have the support he bragged about and the Germans would not put someone with such vile ideas in power anyway. And even if Hitler did actually take over, it is unlikely that he would have power for long. Plotkin even went to hear Goebbels speak to see what the fuss was about and left unimpressed, even stating, "I confess my disappointment. I had come to see a whale and found a minnow." (Nagorski, 79)

This sentiment of Weimar Germany is not unlike the thought of rational Americans today. We underestimated the power of propaganda and the actual fear fake news instills in people. No one thought America would elect the most inept, ill-prepared, hate-filled narcissistic President ever. He has not changed at all since being elected. Trump appears to still embrace the Nazis, even naming one as his top advisor. Thinking Americans are left kicking and screaming while Nazis cheer and threaten our brown-skinned friends. It won't happen here after all.

If one watched and listened to right wing "news", via Fox News, the Patriot Channel on Sirius/XM, or Rush Limbaugh, one would have to believe that elimination of Muslims is the only choice. The vitriol released on Muslims by these people is unending and really unbelievable. This country was founded on freedom of religion. The Founding Fathers did not want to be forced to adhere to a state religion, and they were sure to add the First Amendment to guarantee that for all religions. The amendment reads that "Congress shall make no law respecting an establishment of religion, or prohibiting the free exercise thereof." It is clear. It does not say freedom of Christianity. Islam is a religion. If one has any respect for our Constitution at all, one must defend the right to be Muslim. Not so on the right. The very people that report that liberals want to abolish the Second Amendment – even though they do not – are ready to throw the First Amendment out the window.

Six out of ten people that said they trusted Fox "News" also believed that Islam is trying to establish Sharia law here in the United States. Laura Ingraham, a right-wing pundit on Fox "News", interviewed Daisy Kahn, the wife of Feisal Abdul Rauf, who was building Park51, a Mosque right next to Ground Zero where the September 11, 2001, attacks happened. Ingraham, who is as awful as Coulter, claimed she genuinely liked Mrs. Kahn. However, a few months later she was lamenting the nerve of these awful Muslims having the audacity to build a Mosque (in our country that guarantees freedom of religion)! Fox "News" ran story after story on American citizens erecting a place of worship, namely, Muslims building a mosque. They had 47 guests, 9 of which favored the center. Fair and balanced? You decide. Fox "News" is brilliant at scaring people. The same cited Salon article states:

> In February 2011, the Think Progress website released a study that detailed the specific ways that Fox News manipulates language to insinuate, or in many cases, state explicitly, that Muslims and Islam should be feared. Using three months' worth of material gathered from various television programs from November 2010 to January 2011, a graph was compiled to show that the network disproportionately deployed terms that reflected a negative view of Muslims, more so than Fox News' competitors. For example, Fox used the term "Shariah" 58 times over a three-month period, whereas CNN used the term 21 times, and MSNBC 19 times.

Similarly, Fox hosts brought up the phrases "radical Islam" or "extremist Islam" 107 times in three months, while CNN used the term 78 times and MSNBC only 24 times. Still, Fox used the word "jihad" 65 times, while CNN used it 57 and MSNBC used it 13 times.

Those are scary numbers. And, remember, Fox "News" watchers do not look things up. No matter what Fox says, they believe it, even if it seems impossible. This is demonstrated in the guarantee many Fox "News" watchers gave when Barack Obama was elected President in 2008 that we would be under Sharia Law soon, all because of his Muslim beliefs. Never mind that President Obama is not a Muslim. Never mind that it is perfectly okay for the President of the United States to be Muslim. Fox "News" said he was and, in 2015, 43% of Republicans still believed that. Many Republicans think we need special laws to combat the advent of Sharia Law here. A perfunctory Google search puts that to bed, but as stated previously, Fox "News" watchers do not research. They just go with whatever their "news" channel reports to them as true. They are getting information that coincides with their beliefs, many of which they are learning as Fox "News" tells them what their beliefs are. It is actually a bit bizarre.

Sharia Law is in direct opposition to our Constitution because we allow freedom of religion, any religion, and therefore cannot bind citizens to adhere to any religiously based ideology, including Islam. Amy Smith, in her June 12, 2011, column in USA Today, stated "politicians who cry 'Sharia!' are engaging in one of the oldest and least-proud political traditions — xenophobic demagoguery. One of the easiest ways to spot its use is when politicians carelessly throw around a word simply because it scares some voters." Smith goes on to describe Sharia Law, and it is not even a set of vicious laws, as the right would have you believe. It is a process Muslims and jurists use to help other Muslims make moral decisions. Fox "News" watchers believe we are weeks from having knife-wielding Muslims running around, beheading women for wearing short sleeves. Dick Morris claimed on the Bill O'Reilly Show that Park51, the Mosque at Ground Zero in NYC, was being used to assimilate Muslims and spread Sharia. He may as well have said they are already beheading people in NY.

Some, like the Taliban, take Sharia Law to an insane and dangerous extreme, according to Ms. Smith's article. Any religion is subject to an extreme faction that commits violence in the name of their leader. Christians too. Think of the abortion clinics that are attacked and the doctors murdered. Bill O'Reilly called one such doctor "Tiller the baby killer." That doctor was murdered by a right wing nut job in the name of Jesus. And the right was silent. No reports from the right blaming extreme religious views for mocking our republic and violating Dr. Tiller's constitutional rights. Thinkprogress reported "O'Reilly did briefly say, 'Americans should condemn the murder of Dr. George Tiller," but he then quickly segued into more attacks on Tiller.' But that's not enough. O'Reilly egged his viewers on for months regarding Dr. Tiller, mentioning him specifically 28 times. He was murdered in cold blood on American soil in the name of Jesus Christ for doing his constitutionally guaranteed job.

Part of the problem with the right is their utter inability to distinguish between the 3 billion Muslims in the world and the 42 million members of ISIS. So, on the high side 1.4% of all Muslims are members of ISIS. Ann Coulter uses the terms "ISIS" and "Muslims" interchangeably. She stated, "No more Muslim immigration. How is this making life better for us? But the mass immigration machine churns on … What's the upside of letting millions of Muslims migrate to western countries? 100% of TV talk is @ fighting ISIS–IN SYRIA. Bomb away, but isn't there something else we should consider? Like not letting ISIS move here?" Notice she starts by speaking of Muslims, changing mid-thought, and ends with ISIS. That's called propaganda. Slipping in false narratives. Scary language. Suddenly, people watching cannot distinguish between Muslims and ISIS. They are all the same. Using Coulter's "logic", the Ku Klux Klan has 4 million members and the Republican Party has 62 million members. Therefore, with the Klan occupying fully 6.5% of the Republican Party, can we not interchange "Klan member" with Republicans? "Today, Klan member Paul Ryan introduced a bill to the House." Why not?

Adolf Hitler continuously demonized the Jews in Germany, while pumping up the Aryan population. He was known for getting people fired up in rallies and speeches. His speeches were repetitive nonsense, but they ignited the fear in his followers. Many felt that getting rid of the Jews in Germany was their only lifeline. They were suddenly gravely threatened by the very people they had lived alongside for decades. Jews had been in Germany since 1000 A.D. and were loyal, productive citizens. Hitler believed that Jews were poisoning Germany from inside, just as breast cancer had poisoned his mother 1907. He was utterly paranoid and acted accordingly. He began to transfer this hatred to others and was convincing when he spoke of the inside threat they were invoking to the German government. Part of the lie the anti-Semites told Germans to get them on the side of not only hating Jews but blaming them for the loss of the War was to say they shirked their duties as soldiers. However, 12,000 Jews died fighting in the war. That's approximately 1.7% of the entire Jewish population in Germany. Germany lost approximately 1.7 million Aryan fighters in the war, about 2.5% of their population. That's not a huge difference. They were right there alongside them. But that did not fit Hitler's narrative.

Yet, the anti-Semites like Hitler, Goebbels, and the extreme right wing of the Conservative party needed people to believe otherwise. A study of various positions in the Army was done and afterward, Hitler told the public that the Jews fighting for the Germans were nowhere near the front line. They were hiding in the back letting good, solid Germans do all the hard fighting. No one asked to see the report. They took them at their word. In actuality, the report was found just the opposite, stating that 80% of the Jews in the army were fighting on the front lines. The information from Hitler was entirely fabricated. They lied to push their agenda that the Jews were purposefully ruining Germany. The actual report was never released. Not until 1933 did the leadership in the right wing party of Germany, including Hitler and President Hindenburg, begin to capitalize on the years of propaganda. In 1933 Jews were beginning to be pushed out of public life, no longer working in universities or as attorneys. It was beginning. Their war against the Jews had started, and it would end in 1945 with almost 6 million Jews dead of causes it is difficult to put into words. They were gassed, starved, shot, experimented on, kept in cages, and so many other unspeakable actions.

The American war on Muslims started long before the attacks on the World Trade centers in 2001 and it continues today. Indeed, the anti-Federalists put forth the idea that a Muslim, Jewish American or – gasp! – a Catholic may want to be president someday, and maybe – just maybe – we should have a test to block such an atrocity. For some reason, American Christians think there is a global war against Islam. Americans supported Christians when they rose against Muslim leaders in the Ottomans in the 1800's.Christians believe the "heathens" are trying to convert people to Islam to take over the world. Isn't that what exactly what Christians do? Ever heard of missionaries? Spreading the Good News? Christians believe that only believers in Jesus Christ as savior will achieve eternal life and therefore it is the duty of a Christian to convert non-believers. Why is this different than Muslims trying to get people to believe in Allah? It is not different. At all. Yet Muslims are demonized daily by the right wing "news" outlets.

Glenn Beck has made a name for himself in the right-wing propaganda game by being a Zionist that believes Muslims should not hold office, that most Muslims want Sharia Law, and that10 percent of Muslims are terrorists. For that last claim, he was blasted by scholars that it was just untrue and misleading. Again, the right does not worry about truth; they worry if it fits their narrative. Sharia Law is not dangerous in America. It is a loose set of laws derived from the Quran and Hadith to shape societies. In Muslim societies that adhere to Sharia Law, they use a few of the laws that fit their community. Beck's xenophobic demagoguery shines through. As for Muslims not holding public office, Beck agrees with Republican presidential hopeful Herman Cain, and recent presidential hopeful Ben Carson that Muslims have no place in our government. Our Constitution guarantees them a seat at the table and does not allow for them to be kept out of office based on their religion. It is appalling that anyone can say something in direct conflict with the Constitution and call it American.

This tactic is awfully close to what the Germans did in 1933. Hitler was able to orchestrate laws that forced Jews out of their civil service jobs, university and law court positions, and many other areas of public life. The Nuremburg Laws were enacted in 1935 and were particularly egregious because they did not define Jews by how they practiced, but by the faith of their grandparents. Many people with Jewish grandparents who had converted to Christianity were still caught up in the terror of the Nazis. Between 1937 and 1939, new anti-Jewish regulations segregated Jews further and made daily life very difficult for them. Jews could not attend public schools; go to theaters, cinema, or vacation resorts; or reside or even walk in certain sections of German cities. In America, in 2016, some say we don't want THAT for Muslims. Really? Isn't the current President-Elect talking about banning Muslims, tattooing and monitoring Muslims, and putting them in concentration (internment) camps?

Republican leadership talks about banning Muslims from government, and we are told to "wait and see? Maybe that won't happen." Germany waited and the worst did happen. Hitler did exactly what he said he was going to do. Who is to say that Trump won't as well? He clearly has the backing of the GOP and the right-wing propaganda machine. He is putty in their hands.

A quick look at the demonization and misinformation surrounding Laila Alawa in September 2014 says all we need to know about how the right-wing pundits feel about Muslims. Alawa is an activist and a blogger who was hired by President Obama as a homeland security advisor. She tweeted "9/11 changed the world for good, and there's no other way to say it. I just hope we keep having open conversations about our differences." Innocuous, right? It's definitely a true statement with a little hope tacked on to the end – until the right-wing propaganda machine twisted her words into what seemed like cheerleading for the perpetrators of those attacks. In 2016 Pamela Geller wrote, after she was hired by Obama: Obama's Homeland Security Advisor is [a] Syrian MIGRANT who CHEERS 9/11, it CHANGED THE WORLD FOR THE GOOD." Notice anything different about Alawa's tweet and what Islamophobe Geller reported it to be? Geller inserted the word "the" before "good" and effectually changed the meaning of the entire tweet. "For good" is a known American phrase to mean permanently. Example: I hope that dog stays off our lawn for good. Unfortunately, that did not match the agenda of Geller and others, so they added the word "the" changing the meaning to "for the better." And their followers were none the wiser. Other propaganda sites followed suit: Freedom

Daily: "Obama Hires Muslim Who Praised 9/11 Attacks – Puts Her on Homeland Security Committee" and "Just After Orlando, Obama Hires Muslim Who Praised 9/11 for This Job!" If one was to follow only right wing "news", their narrative was verified time and time again. They did not need to research it themselves. Alawa simply stated that the attacks on the World Trade Centers made an effective and permanent change in the world in which we live. She was right.

Fake news has been in America forever. Most elections have had some form of propaganda that influenced a few people. It is arguable that in 2016 the difference was the speed at which millions received and disseminated fake news that changed the game. Donald Trump tweeted: *In addition to winning the Electoral College in a landslide, I won the popular vote if you deduct the millions of people who voted illegally.* Within hours headlines read "Trump Tweets Millions Voted Illegally for Clinton" and none that read "Trump Lies and Says Illegal Aliens Voted." Never mind that the initial information came from Infowars.com, likely one of the more bizarre websites where Trump gleans fake news consistently. The point is, the next day I heard people arguing that Donald Trump actually did not lose the popular vote by more than 2.5 million votes because you have to take away Hillary Clinton's illegal voters. CNN's Alison Camerota interviewed Trump supporters who claimed "the media said people voted illegally" and "Obama said illegals could vote this year." When asked where they saw this, after her literal face palm, Camerota found the Fox "news" channel had deceptively edited a video of Obama to make it appear that he said illegal immigrants could vote, when the transcripts told a totally different story. These

Trump supporters just believed what they were told. No research, no getting to the original source of the statement, just blindly following Dear Leader Trump.

## Chapter 4

*You know, it really doesn't matter what the media write as long as you've got a young, and beautiful piece of ass.* – Donald Trump

Propaganda starts from a false premise. In the case of 1920's and 1930's Germany that premise was that Jews and other groups are threatening the existence and lifestyle of pure blooded Germans. The Nazi party was a brand new political group based on German Nationalism and anti-Semitism. They were a rag-tag group of unemployed soldiers, the SS, who were impossibly loyal to their leader. In November 1923 they attempted a coup d'etat in Munich, which became known as the Beer Hall Putsch. It was a colossal failure and Hitler was sentenced to 5 years in prison. He spent less than a year there and, in the meantime, wrote his autobiography, Mein Kampf, or My Struggle, which captured a lonely, troubled man with lofty goals to rule the world and rid it of Jews and non-Germans. This actually solidified his role on the national stage and gave him a platform to spread his vitriol. Germany was reeling from the loss of World War I and was in financial disarray. The political parties were in tatters, with splinter groups throughout and no one group really having a clear hold on power.

The Reichstag Fire of 1933 produced the Reichstag Fire Decree, which was the beginning of total dictatorship for Adolf Hitler. He convinced Hindenburg that total control was necessary to protect the German people. This included the suspended right to assembly, freedom of speech, freedom of the press, and other constitutional protections, including all restraints on police investigation. Hitler used a demonstrable lie to obtain absolute power. Looking back, one could say that there was an event, the fire, which allowed a reasonable response to protect the people. But there had to be a premise to sell this idea. The communists already had to be demonized in order to sell this idea so quickly. By suspending freedom of the press, Hitler and his party controlled the information available to the German people. It is much easier to make your point when no one is challenging you. The newspapers began to run only pro-Third Reich articles and ran negative – and often false – stories about Jews, the disabled, and homosexuals. (Nagorski, 48)

Donald Trump started to suppress information when he was running for President and has continued the effort since being elected. During the time up to the election, Trump had the press corps assigned to his campaign held in "pens" at rallies and encouraged his followers to verbally attack them. At a rally in Cincinnati, the press had to exit through a back door and have a motorcade escort them to safety. Reporters suffered through chants of "CNN sucks" and "tell the truth," had items thrown at them, and were personally threatened by people at Trump rallies. The President-Elect not only encouraged this despicable behavior, he offered to pay attorney's fees for the Trump supporters who may be arrested for their behavior. Interestingly, post-election research shows the media wrote many more negative stories about Trump's opponent, Hillary Clinton, than they did Trump. But that truth does not matter. Trump stated the stories about him were false, and that is all of his followers needed to know. It didn't matter that he said it and it was recorded on tape. It didn't matter it was in court documents. Trump said it was false and therefore it was. Fact checking be damned.

Donald Trump also promised to "open up libel laws" in order to make it easier for him to sue the major media corporations that were saying bad things about him. Let us not forget that this is a man that published false information about the current President, Barack Obama, stating he was not born in America. Patently false. In print – the very definition of libel. The President said nothing and simply produced his birth certificate. Now Trump wants to make it impossible for the press to write anything negative about him while he is President, lest they be sued. The First Amendment of our Constitution guarantees freedom of the press. Lincoln University stated Freedom of the Press "protects the right to obtain and publish information or opinions without government censorship or fear of punishment. Censorship occurs when the government examines and produces and prohibits the use of material it finds offensive." So Donald Trump is unaware of the First Amendment? Does he think the President can do whatever he wants, like Hitler? He needs to censor the news? Is he hiding something? Why does the dissemination of information scare him? These questions and more deserve answers as Donald Trump stomps on the very freedoms he was elected to defend.

Adolf Hitler quickly changed Germany to a one-party system, disallowing competing political parties. Taking over the presses of now-illegal parties and controlling the information was integral in getting support for his ideas.

Hitler had bad ideas. He wanted to rid the world of Jews, disabled people, and homosexuals. He wanted world domination for Germans, whom he believed to be the greatest of all races. Upon taking over the presses, Goebbels took over and spread Hitler's ideas far and wide in Germany. Messages were sent to American soldiers and other Allied Forces by air dropping leaflets. The new rules were harsh, and long-term family-owned presses fell into the hands of the Nazis. The Holocaust Museum reports:

> "Under the new Editors Law of October 4, 1933, the association kept registries of "racially pure" editors and journalists, and excluded Jews and those married to Jews from the profession. Propaganda Ministry officials expected editors and journalists, who had to register with the Reich Press Chamber to work in the field, to follow the mandates and instructions handed down by the ministry. In paragraph 14 of the law, the regime required editors to omit anything "calculated to weaken the strength of the Reich abroad or at home."

There was to be no negative news about the Third Reich, Hitler, or any of his ideas. He was a dictator with all the power of information – and controlling information is everything.

Donald Trump has controlled the media during the run up to the election and certainly after. Again, most on the right do not seem to think the President-Elect shunning or controlling the media coverage of him is a problem. I repeat, those who ignore history dare repeat it. In June 2016, Trump revoked the credentials of The Washington Post, mainly because the newspapers weren't saying nice things about him. Here's his post about the revocation:

> "Based on the incredibly inaccurate coverage and reporting of the record setting Trump campaign, we are hereby revoking the press credentials of the phony and dishonest Washington *Post*," he wrote in a Facebook post.

Never mind that he announced it on Facebook like a teenager. The press said something with which he did not agree and he barred them from doing their job of informing the American people. It is really embarrassing. And dangerous. The Post responded in kind and has continued coverage of the President-Elect. But the words that Editor Martin Baron used were powerful. He wrote:

> "Donald Trump's decision to revoke *The Washington Post's* press credentials is nothing less than a repudiation of the role of a free and independent press. When coverage doesn't correspond to what the candidate wants it to be, then a news organization is banished. The Post will continue to cover Donald Trump as it has all along—honorably, honestly, accurately, energetically, and unflinchingly. We're proud of our coverage, and we're going to keep at it."

He also disallowed the Des Moines Register. Reporters from Politico and Buzzfeed and a *New York Times* journalist have all been barred from Trump events. So much for free press.

Trump did say he would not pull press credentials once he was elected to be President, if in fact he was elected. Well, he was elected. Traditionally, the newly elected President holds a press conference within a few days of the election. He talks about how proud of his voters he is, how he or she will be a president for all the people and to lay out his or her hopes and dreams for the future of our great country. They inform the press of their travels and the reporters duly report the comings and goings of our new President-Elect. That is, until now. Trump has already halted any coverage of him or his plans. He has skirted the press and not held a press conference since July, let alone a post-election press conference. Bill Clinton waited nine days to have a press conference. At the time of this writing of this book, it has been 22 days since Donald Trump was elected. And the American people are in the dark. Sure, Trump would have to answer tough questions about his conflicts of interest, his reneging on every campaign promise he made before the votes were even fully counted, and his many missteps with people who are not white – but that is what the President of the United States of America does, answers hard questions. For four years. Donald Trump has not even put his hand on the Bible yet, and he is cowering from the very people that keep our Republic sound with information.

In the early 1930's, Adolf Hitler was displeased with the media attention he was getting, much like Trump is today. Hitler's solution was to turn the weekly Nazi propaganda paper, *Volkischer Beobachter,* into a daily publication, guaranteeing the news he wanted out into Germany was timely. He eventually took over all the information in Germany. He censored books by Jewish people and any books that put Jews or non-Germans in a positive light, and he pushed books that praised him and his army or that spoke disparagingly of Jews. This included all the books and information in the education system of Germany, therefore, everything the students learned about Hitler and the Nazis was all positive, and everything they learned about Jews was designed to cause fear and hate. His purpose was to garner blind obedience of the German people. Therefore no matter what he did, he earned the consent of the German people who had bought into his propaganda machine. The regime perpetrated and encouraged violence against Jews, initially verbally, then through newspapers and pamphlets. Eventually, the vitriol would turn into actual random physical acts of violence against Jews. They were beaten in the street, their property was damaged, and they were humiliated for no reason, other than that they were Jewish. (Goldhagen, 136)

The Aryan Germans had been radicalized, meaning to cause someone to support a radical political or social idea. They were supporting the elimination and persecution of an entire race of people based on what they were reading and listening to on the radio. They were their lifelong neighbors, yet the Nazis told them to be fearful of Jews. And there was no counter argument. No one was saying the Jews are just as they have always been. There was no news to say that the financial crisis was worldwide and that it was not the Jews fault.

The right-wing media in America has radicalized their listeners as well. They have absolutely demonized Muslims, Mexicans, Gays, and really anyone who is not conservative and white. Attacks on Muslims, Mexicans and those in the LGBTQ community in the United States have skyrocketed since Trump was elected. Over 900 incidences of hate crimes go almost unnoticed on Fox "news," infowars.com, and Breitbart. The violence and spray painted swastikas on churches do not even get a mention. A female, Muslim New York City police officer was picking up her child at school and was harassed and told to go back from where she came because now that Trump was in charge, she was going to be deported. Another woman wearing a hijab was pushed down the steps of the subway in NYC because she was wearing a hijab. Latino school children are being told by their school mates that they were going to be deported.

In another incident, on December 4, 2016, a man walked into Comet Ping Pong, a pizza joint in Washington, D.C., with a semi-automatic rifle in hopes of single-handedly breaking up a child sex ring run by Hillary Clinton. And that's not a joke. An actual "news" story on fake Web sites spread around and somehow, someway this guy thought he was going to save all of these kids who were supposedly part of a child sex ring. Any cognitive, thinking person would read such a story and think, if that were true the police would certainly already be there. But these people have been radicalized. They have been given information contrary to common sense and, because they have been told over and over and over again that the "main stream media" is lying to them, they believe every word. They are in fact the only Americans with valid information. They say the main stream media is lying and they are the only ones with the truth. It is truly cult like and scary. On December 7, 2016, a Florida woman, Lucy Richards, was indicted on four counts of transmitting threats because she was harassing a parent whose child was killed in the mass shooting in Sandy Hook Elementary School in Newtown, CT, four years ago. Richards believes the Web site infowars.com and its founder, Alex Jones, when he claims Sandy Hook was a hoax. Unbelievable.

Interestingly, most right-wing propaganda watchers are completely ignorant to the fact they are being bamboozled. Likewise, once Hitler had their ear and was spoon feeding the residents of Germany information, they no longer questioned his motives or means or end game. Since the 2016 general election, America has seen that with Trump as well. One of the right-wing mantras during the campaign for President was that Trump's opponent, Hillary Clinton had not held a presser and was unavailable and unwilling to talk to the press. Trump has not held a press conference since July 27, 2016. One hundred and thirty-one days. And not a peep from the right. Clinton was crucified for the lack of access for the press. The right said she was afraid of the press and did not want to answer questions about her many "scandals" – all of which were fabricated. (We will explore the demonization of Hillary Clinton later in this effort.) However, Trump does not have to answer questions from the press. As a matter of fact he is applauded by the right for manipulation of the press and NOT informing them of his next move or any of the day-to-day functions of the President-Elect, a complete break from the usual protocol. They think he is really handing it to the press that used his own words to lie about him. Part of being a victim of propaganda is when the truth is right there, the duped still cannot see it. For instance, Donald Trump tweeted, *"The concept of global warming was created by and for the Chinese."* When Clinton said so much in the debates, he literally denied his own words. He said, "I never said that." Yet his followers believed him.

Part of the problem is that Trump has an insatiable need to be liked. When people praise him, he considers them good and worthy of his attentions, even if they are ruthless dictators that happen to be enemies of America, like Vladimir Putin. On December 6, 2016, Trump tweeted, *"If the press would cover me accurately and honestly, I would have far less reason to "tweet." Sadly, I don't know if that will happen."* Trump, the most unpopular president ever to win the Presidential Election, lost the popular by 2.7 million votes to the Electoral College loser, Hillary Clinton. The most unpopular president-elect ever wants the press to say only nice things about him. If the press will not say nice things about him, he will still get the information out he wants the people to know, via Twitter. Just like Hitler needed to control the narrative, so does Trump. And his followers are not questioning it at all. In fact, they think it is a show of strength. They appear to believe that he is really giving the press what they deserve, telling all those bad, but true, stories about him during the campaign. He is really showing them! Sadly, Hitler really showed them, too. People were told only what he wanted them to hear, and they believed the Jews were taking over the world and trying to thin the strong German bloodline. They really believed extermination of the Jews meant survival of their own culture and race. Just like the right believes Donald Trump is going to save them from (insert scary race, economic crisis, progressives, and socialists here).

Freedom of press and access to the President are vital to American culture and rule by the people for the people. If our President is operating in secrecy, we have no recourse when our country goes in a direction we were not intending when we elected him. Part of American protocol to keep the peace and to keep our Republic functioning and knowledgeable is access. If the press cannot ask the President questions and weigh in on concerning decisions, we have no Republic. We have a President acting individually and separately from the people. America has an autocrat in President-Elect Trump, someone who insists on obedience from others and is domineering. He is insisting the press cover him the way he wants to be covered, and if they do not do as he wishes, they get no coverage at all. He insults the press for simply reporting the news and insists they change the story to fit his narrative, whether it is truthful or not. Presidents have always been under the microscope of the press, favorably and unfavorably, and none has discontinued contact nor scolded the press for not saying what put the president in the best light. We have a problem America, and that problem is Donald Trump. He is showing all the signs and insecurities of the likes of Adolf Hitler, and almost 40 percent of us are praising him for it. It truly is scary.

## Chapter 5

*The leader of genius must have the ability to make different opponents appear as if they belonged to one category.* – Adolf Hitler

Propaganda often vilifies a large group of people who are perceived to be threatening the very existence and lifestyle of a superior group. Hitler used the Jews and homosexuals as his scapegoat. There have been many theories floated to explain Hitler's hatred of Jews. The most prominent and the one he spells out himself in <u>Mein Kampf</u> is that the Jews were responsible for Germany's loss and economic downfall in WWI. He attributed the influence of the Jews in each of the political and influential parties in Germany to the mistakes that accounted for the superior people, the Germans, loss and worldwide humiliation in the Great War. Often historians put a personal spin on Hitler's views and his treatment of Jews. His treatment and extermination was over the top. For that reason, people try to attribute his hatred as less strategic and more of a payback. Maybe. But for the purposes of explaining his use of propaganda, this effort will save that exploration for a later date.

One of the methods for a successful propaganda effort is to make a group of people feel superior to others. One wants to save their exceptional race or religion at the expense of another because of perceived threats. Hitler's mentor, Dietrich Eckhart, was one of the men who started the Nazi Party and was a member of the Thule Society. The Thule Society was founded on the theory of racial purity. It had an originalist viewpoint of Germanic culture. The

Society was a secret group of occultists who believed in the coming of a "German Messiah" who would redeem Germany after its defeat in World War I, and blamed democratic socialist and Jews for Germany's defeat in WWI. Basically if you did not have original German blood in your veins, you were less than others and on the list to be exterminated. The Thule Society was founded on the principle of genetic superiority. When one joined the Thule Society, he had to sign an oath stating: *"The signer hereby swears to the best of his knowledge and belief that no Jewish or coloured blood flows in either his or in his wife's veins, and that among their ancestors are no members of the coloured races."*

The Thule Society had its own newspaper, the *Münchener Beobachter or* the Munich Observer. The Munich Observer later became the *Volkischer Beobachter,* the People's Observer, which you may recall was the weekly newspaper Hitler turned into a daily in 1923. Adolf Hitler bought into the ideas of the Thule Society hook, line, and sinker. He actually believed Germans had superior genes and that they should be the powerful race in the world; that Aryan Germans were truly the master race. Hitler truly believed in eugenics and Aryan Germans were actually Nordic Aryans. Hitler believed Nordic Aryans to be the greatest race of all time and therefore the only race fit to rule the world. To that point, Aryan Germans could not mix bloodlines, so Hitler developed a tool to make sure they were pure. Any Aryan German could get a certificate if they could prove that all four of their grandparents were German and were baptized in a Christian church. People with these certificates could marry and continue the strong bloodlines of the master race. Of course, Hitler was crazy with power and the result of trying to save their superior gene resulted in the extermination of Jews. (Hamerow, 293) Nordic Aryans believed that political boundaries should mirror these alleged racial and ethnic groups, thus justifying ethnic cleansing in order to achieve "racial purity" and also to achieve ethnic homogeneity in the nation-state.

Steve Bannon believes in eugenics, just as Hitler did. A former colleague of Bannon's, Julia Jones, recounted her interactions with Bannon to reporter Scott Shane:

"Mr. Bannon occasionally talked about the genetic superiority of some people and once mused about the desirability of limiting the vote to property owners." Bannon went on to say that his theory did exclude his African American assistant, Wendy, because she was family. Racists often point to having African American friends or colleagues. Being friendly with them only proves they are not racists. Journalist Brittany King stated, "Knowing a black person, smiling at a black person, and even hiring a black person are not reasons to ignore the problematic things that happen to black people on a daily basis." The theory is akin to randomly shooting animals but claiming to be an animal lover because you are vegan. It is simply illogical, and one does not nullify the other. On the contrary, it is one the tenants of racism to single a few "good ones" out while vilifying the group. There was an African American at one of Trump's rallies and he said, "Look at my African American!" Remember, after Donald Trump said Mexico was sending over its worst, the criminals and the rapists, he finished it up by saying, "some I assume are good people." And, you guessed it, Donald

Trump firmly believes his superior genes got him and his children where they are today. He claims his children are set to do well in this world because of their genetics, which are, of course, inherited from him. In a speech in South Carolina, Trump mentioned his uncle to reiterate his belief in his good genetics, stating "my uncle was a great professor and scientist and engineer, Dr. John Trump at MIT; good genes, very good genes." He has stated before that he feels like he was bred like a racehorse. Having this superior genetic disposition that makes one better not because of effort but because they were born better is a hallmark of white nationalism.

Not only do white supremacists use propaganda to talk about how much better they are than everyone else, they talk about how much better their followers are than all these lesser races. Hitler historian Goetz Aly said Hitler was a "feel-good Dictator," making German people feel important and cared for by their Fuhrer. The entire ideology that involved making Jewish Germans feel terrible was designed to also make non-Jewish Germans feel better. The rationing system, the identifying marks, and no longer shopping at Jewish-owned shops was all an effort to raise Aryan Germans up while making Jewish Germans feel less hopeful and weak. And, in Hitler's mind, the weak needed to be defeated. In a speech in Munich on April 13, 1923, Hitler shouted, "THE WHOLE WORLD OF NATURE IS A MIGHTY STRUGGLE BETWEEN STRENGTH AND WEAKNESS - AN ETERNAL VICTORY OF THE STRONG OVER THE WEAK." So he set Aryan Germans up to succeed, all while setting others up to fail, a means of making the Germans feel stronger and better than their non-Aryan countryman.

His speeches were designed to make Aryan Germans feel superior and give them the confidence to help Hitler eliminate the vermin he thought the Jews to be.

Donald Trump uses the same tactics in his speeches. Though his followers are notably less educated than the rest of the nation, with most of them holding a high school diploma or less, he tells them they are smart. In a speech in Nashville, Tennessee, in August, Trump took the opportunity to again emphasize the importance of his supporters. He attributed his continued lead in Republican primary polls to the intelligence of his supporters. He said, "The reason is people in this country are smart. They don't believe a lot of what they see in the media." This statement verifies two aspects of effective propaganda. First, telling your followers they are smarter than everyone validates them and keeps them coming back for more – much like the "feel good" fuhrer Adolf Hitler did. Secondly, he tells these very smart people they are smart for believing him and not the newspapers and radio shows that are saying bad things about him. All of the "bad news" about Trump was true, of course, but he told them it was all fabricated. And his followers believed him. Never mind it was his voice on the tape discussing the sexual assault of women, and they knew it was true. But, they were feeling good about being so smart, and this just further validated their efforts.

As did Adolf Hitler, Donald Trump struggles with criticism and not being liked. Hitler was extremely self-conscious about his appearance. He had wide hips, thin shoulders, an ill-shaped face and head, and walked with a very feminine gait. It is said that he would not have made his own army because of the strict height and proportion regulations he required for the SA. He wore clothes to hide his body, with rumors that he wore padded clothes to accentuate the areas in which he felt really inferior. Hitler practiced his speeches for hours. He knew he could be a great orator, but he needed to sound powerful too, which he simply was not. So he worked hard with a photographer to stand and look and gesture in the right direction to make himself seem more imposing than he was. He was a great showman.

From the beginning of Hitler's rule in 1933, he suppressed open criticism. There is a long list of people who attempted to come out against Hitler, such as Alfred Delp and Bernhard Lichtenberg. These two men were executed for plotting against the fuhrer. Hitler's inferiority complex started as a young child. He always thought highly of stronger kids, even though he was not one, and learned to feel superior. He needed to find kids on the playground that he was bigger and stronger than. Again, he was not an imposing figure; he simply fought and played with younger, smaller kids in order to feel superior. Later in life, contributing to his sense of inferiority, Hitler was not accepted into art school. He used this opportunity to hone his painting skills and was said to have made himself into a very good painter. But he could not just change the fact that he did not have broad shoulders, or that he was below average in height, or that he had a tick that made his lip curl uncontrollably. To combat these inefficiencies, he became the fuhrer and attempted to rule the world. As you do.

When comparing Trump and Hitler, there is a challenge in discussing how they each individually handled criticism. Hitler was a virtual unknown that no one thought would actually come into power, and after coming into power he did not allow dissent. So no one was legitimately publicly critical in the early years. And once he became dictator, being critical meant execution sometimes coupled with torture. Trump's reaction to criticism is much better documented. He does most of his criticism on the open format of Twitter, so a simple examination of his Twitter account often reveals the people who have criticized him most recently. Of course, traditional news sources report facts like Donald Trump will not release his taxes or Donald Trump said, "Grab women by the pussy" to journalist Billy Bush, or Donald Trump cheats contractors or any number of easily proved accusations, and Trump accuses them of lying or being overly critical of him.

Not long after the general election and after a deeply scrutinized "deal" with United Technologies, the parent company of Carrier, Trump went after their Union leader, Chuck Jones. Jones had stated they were largely left out of the deal and that the Union did not get a fair chance to represent their workers fairly and that the deal did not do all Trump said it did. Trump, obviously attempting to stifle challenges and reduce insubordination, blasted him on Twitter stating, " *Chuck Jones, who is President of United Steelworkers 1999, has done a terrible job representing workers. No wonder companies flee country!"* Trump followed that tweet up an hour later by tweeting, "*If United Steelworkers 1999 was any good, they would have kept those jobs in Indiana. Spend more time working - less time talking. Reduce dues"* The truth is, Jones was correct. The deal was not a good deal for workers at all. Only 850 jobs were saved, 2,100 Carrier jobs are still moving to Mexico. The deal cost tax payers $7 million. That is $7 million tax payers are giving to a company that profited over $2 billion in their climate controls section of their business model alone. The unions worked tirelessly with Carrier to keep their jobs here, but Carrier was not swayed. They can pay Mexican workers $2-to$3 in Mexico, and union members were making $22 an hour in Indianapolis. Carrier also stated, after successfully dealing with Trump out of 7 million tax payer dollars, that the jobs they left in Indiana would likely be lost to automation within the year. Essentially Trump paid for their research to get their automation off the ground so robots can take over the jobs Trump saved. The "Art of the Deal" does not seem that artful, does it?

Trump is also adept at making his thin-skinned retorts to people criticizing him as doing something great for Americans, as opposed to just trying to having an eighth-grade response to someone disagreeing with him. Trump also makes his tireless eighth-grade twitter responses seem like he is really helping Americans, when he is really just having a thin-skinned, knee jerk retort to criticism. Take his tweet last week about Boeing for example: *"Boeing is building a brand new 747 Air Force One for future presidents, but costs are out of control, more than $4 billion. Cancel order!"* First of all, the information is incorrect. Boeing actually has a $176 million deal with the United States to research improvements for Air Force One with the United States Air Force. Also, Trump spins this as some government waste and he is going to make America great again by making a better deal. In actuality, the CEO of Boeing was very critical of Trump challenging long-standing diplomatic norms with China and it hurting Boeing and other international companies who sell to China billions of dollars' worth of goods. The article was in the Chicago Tribune and Trump was tweeting within hours trying to harm Boeing, clearly retribution for going against "Dear Leader." Air Force Secretary Deborah Lee Jones put out a statement stating that Air Force One is much more than a commercial airliner, therefore the costs of the two should not be compared. Senator Patty Murray, a Democrat from Washington, where Boeing operates in the United States said, "I hope the president-elect takes the time to talk to the Pentagon and the Air Force and Boeing about how defense contracts work before he tweets." He does not and he will not. He is a willful, petulant man-child that knows more than everyone else anyway – at least according to him.

Donald Trump's thin skin is also evident when discussing how much he lost the popular vote by in the election. He lost by much more than any Electoral College winner in history, over 2.7 million votes. He is the least popular president ever to be President-Elect, with approval ratings hovering in the mid-forties. Compared to the same point during his post-election in 2008, Barack Obama had approval ratings in the seventies. Trump struggles mightily with the fact that almost 3 million more people voted for Clinton. He actually staid there must have been fraudulent votes for his opponent. He tweeted, *"In addition to winning the Electoral College in a landslide, I won the popular vote if you deduct the millions of people who voted illegally."* This statement is completely false, yet after he tweeted it out, his supporters restated it as truth. It is ridiculous. His Electoral College win ranked 46th out of 58 presidential elections. So saying he won in a landslide is just embarrassing. We can use Google. Trump got the information from infowars.com, a propaganda Web site run by the craziest of all the crazies, Alex Jones. This is not his first mention in this book, and likely won't be his last. At any rate, he attributed the news to a Web site that claims to have not reported the initial lie that 3 million undocumented people voted. It does not matter to Donald Trump, or to Trump's followers, that he lied and that there is no evidence to even somewhat support his statement. They will never look it up or suspect anything at all, because it supports the narrative of Ann Coulter and Sean Hannity and everyone else on Fox "news" that democrats let Mexicans in to get votes and water down the Caucasian bloodline. Ridiculous. There is zero evidence. None. It is completely fabricated, yet Trump apologists and Fox "news" watchers repeat it as if it's gospel.

The stories of Trump's inadequacies and his childlike responses to them are endless. It is important to remember that Trump's signaling out people who criticize him to be harassed by his supporters is not unlike how Hitler behaved in Germany. Hitler basically turned the SA loose on the people he had condemned through propaganda, allowing them to beat up harass and vilify them. Journalist Knickerbocker stated, "The nation turned into a huge hunting party and for a fortnight all attention was absorbed in chasing the Jews." Journalist Abraham Plotkin, an American, wrote, "The Nazis have turned loose forces they themselves do not understand." (Nagorski 106) One can hope that Trump also does not understand the viciousness in which his supporters lash out to those that oppose and are exposed by Trump. Union leader Chuck Jones has had death threats. He has had people tell him they know where he lives and what kind of car he drives. He also stated that after exposing Donald Trump as a liar, most of Trump's followers dismiss that by saying things like, "He got the numbers mixed up." Someone who, by his own barometer, is the best negotiator in the world, got his numbers mixed up? Negotiators know the numbers. Stop making excuses for Donald Trump when he is wrong. Just say he is wrong or lying.

This brings us to a third point, that of the cult-like following of both Donald Trump and Adolf Hitler. Many people in Germany thought Hitler may even be the Messiah. No kidding. Most of the fanatical followers of the Third Reich thought Hitler to be a messiah sent by God (Nagorski, 168) American journalist William Shirer saw Hitler gaining fanatical admiration. He likened the people coming out to support the Fuhrer as a hysterical mob. "They looked up at him as if he were a Messiah, their faces transformed into something positively inhuman." (173) Then-journalist Shirer, and future Director of the CIA, Richard Helms, were riding in a limousine behind Hilter's at one parade and stated:

> There was, I must admit, something mesmerizing about this ride… However much one loathed Nazis, and I certainly did, this was heady stuff. There could be no question about the German people's intoxication with their leader.

One definition of cult is: *a misplaced or excessive admiration for a particular person or thing.* Excessive admiration. It seems the true followers of Hitler certainly had excessive admiration for him. And because of the propaganda machine, they were able to justify or overlook all the horrific ideas Hitler was pushing for Germany.

Donald Trump's followers also have a fanatical view of their leader. They are just as crazy as Nazis when it comes to defending the President-Elect. While campaigning for the presidency, Trump did things that would have torpedoed any candidate without a total cult following. One of the more egregious comments, because of the GOP's self-proclaimed commitment to the military and veterans (a quick look at blocked spending for vets over the last eight years nullifies that notion, but again, the right does not investigate and I digress) was when Donald Trump said Senator John McCain was not a war hero because he was captured. Apparently, as he stated himself, he likes veterans that were not captured. That flies in the face of everything American and especially if one has even an ounce of respect for our troops. But the response was not the vitriol one would expect when someone attacks a decorated veterans of was in this country.

Rush Limbaugh defended Trump by using the ever reliable, "but-democrats-do-it-too!" defense, siting a speech in 2002 by Democratic Senator from Minnesota Al Franken in which he said almost the same thing. Must be true, right? Where was your outrage then democrats? Gotcha!

However, Limbaugh fails to tell his audience, who do no research whatsoever, that Al Franken is a former comedian for "Saturday Night Live" and that his comments were at an event at which he was the comedic speaker meant to entertain, and those statements were all in jest. He was supposed to make people laugh, and if you put it in context, it is quite funny. Ann Coulter, on Fox "news" on July 20, 2015, defended Trump by calling Republicans "midgets" for jumping all over Trump's off-hand remarks about Sen. John McCain's war record when they themselves have said far worse things. Little people slur aside (it is Coulter after all), one does not get to disparage the service of a decorated service member, five-year POW and long-time Senator because this one time, someone said something even meaner! We are not in eighth grade, and the GOP needs to let their pundits know it. The real problem is that Coulter says these things, while Fox viewers are thinking, wow – maybe Trump should not have said that, and they think, oh, no, it is ok. Coulter "Fox-splained" it to us. Dear Leader is still the chosen one.

Dim-witted former Governor of Alaska and Trump supporter, Sarah Palin suggested that God chose Trump for the American people. Her bizarre interview on Breitbart's morning "news" broadcast was reported by Independent.uk like this:

"No doubt, divine providence played a huge role in this election, I will boldly proclaim that. I saw it first-hand. I was there on the campaign trail. I saw how things were changing. I saw more and more people's eyes open, and I think so much of that was based on the church in general, those people of faith who were praying to God that people would wake up. Remember, our Founders dedicated this land, this new country that would be America, this idea of America, dedicated it to God. If I were President, I'd re-dedicate us to God."

It's just bizarre that she would think like this. Or is it? Similarly whacky Michelle Bachmann also stated she thought the God had chosen the non-church-attending, Playboy cover star and thrice married fornicator Donald Trump to morally lead this great nation back to the God he never worshiped. And that God had chosen him to do just that. It is similar to picking rapist Mike Tyson as your anti-rape spokesperson.

The idea that only Donald Trump can be America's savior was initially spread by none other than, you guessed it, Donald Trump. At the Republican National Convention on July 21, 2016, Trump stated, "No one knows the system better than me, which is why I alone can fix it." Anyone living in a constitutional republic, as we are in America, should be alarmed by that assertion. Our leaders are bound by constraints to keep that very thing from happening. But the right really does see him as some sort of messiah that is going to save America by destroying the very threads that hold us together. Indira A.R. Lakshmanan of the Boston Globe reported on July 22, 2016, that this worldview looks more like that of various dictators around the world, not the leader of the leading Democratic Republic in the world. And Trump's sentiment – "America First" – is a scary reminder of Nazi Germany, where Aryan Germans' rights and privileges were thought of above common decency. On July 28, 2016, Hillary Clinton, Trump's democratic opponent for the presidency, stated, "don't trust anyone who says 'I alone can fix it.'" Wouldn't it have been nice if some Americans had heeded the words of the most qualified person ever to run for president?

**Chapter 6**

*I've said if Ivanka weren't my daughter, perhaps I'd be dating her.* – Donald Trump


For propaganda to have its desired effect, the media and the public must be complicit in different ways. The media must report the falsehoods as truth, at least on some outlets, and the public must be willing to gather its information solely from propagandist's sources and ignore the rest as false or coddling the enemy. Often, at least one or many media sources are promoting the party attempting to use propaganda. They begin to be a resource for spreading falsehoods and demeaning other news sources as false and catering to the perceived enemy. Only 3% of the newspapers in Germany were Nazi-friendly in the 1920's. The other news sources were not overly concerned with an extreme right-wing party whose stated goals were to eradicate from Germany an entire religion. But that 3% was enough to get a fringe following that resulted in enough backing to help the party soar to prominence by the early 1930's. By the time Hitler took over the free press in 1934, the propaganda wheel was rolling full steam ahead.

Hitler did not need a complicit media; he forced a complicit media. He was a dictator that took over the information Germans received and made sure it fit his agenda. If anyone went against him, they were found, tortured, and executed. Donald Trump, as yet, does not yield that sort of power. There is still Freedom of the Press in America, which for some means the freedom to spread propaganda that suits their political agenda. In 2016 the media was fixated on the ratings that were produced by putting Donald Trump's face and words on screens across the country. They did not challenge his many lies nor did they stick with some of tasks we normally ask of our journalists. Trump repeated several times that he would produce his tax returns, and the media never pushed him on it. He stated that every single one of the nine different women accusing him of sexual assault was lying, and no one asked him about it in detail. He attacks regular citizens on Twitter and no one asks him why he thinks that is an attribute of someone that should run the free world. There were so many unanswered questions about our President-Elect; it seems the media just allowed itself to be bowled over by a bully. That bully was Donald Trump.

It seems Donald Trump had control of the media from the beginning of his campaign. Nicholas Kristoff wrote an article for the *New York Times* in March 2016 attributing some of Trump's rise to the top of the Republican nominee for President to the media. He claimed the first big failing of corporate media was not fact checking Donald Trump when he made outrageous claims, such as Wisconsin's effective unemployment rate was 20 percent. It was actually around five percent, but that went unchecked and "Trumpers" nationwide parroted the bad information. The reason we have interviews of people running for public office is to ask questions, get the answers, and get the truth. If the media fails to say, "Hey, that is not a true statement," they are doing us a disservice. As a matter of fact, they admit to doing themselves a disservice. Kristoff added:

"Trump is not just an instant ratings/circulation/clicks gold mine; he's the motherlode," Ann Curry, the former "Today" anchor, told me. "He stepped on to the presidential campaign stage precisely at a moment when the media is struggling against deep insecurities about its financial future. The truth is, the media has needed Trump like a crack addict needs a hit."

So, the ratings of various media outlets superseded finding a qualified President of the United States? Noted.

In the same article, the *New York Times* found that Donald Trump received $1.9 billion worth of free press. The man that bragged about funding his own campaign had to spend only $10 million to get $1.9 billion worth of media time. That's far more time than any of his opponents received. Of course, they were not money makers. Hillary Clinton and his republican primary opponents spoke like boring politicians. They talked about poverty and the economy and foreign and domestic issues - issues that people generally do not put much effort into learning about or care about hearing about. But Donald Trump! He was saying things like, "I will make Mexico pay!" and "I know more than the Generals" and "I know more about ISIS than anyone!" He was outrageous and gregarious and he flirted with everyone and discredited the very media that was giving him all the free coverage. We all stopped and watched the train wreck that was Donald Trump's candidacy, and he crashed his way right into the presidency.

Donald Trump was, and still is, so ill-informed about the issues and the way our government runs, it was actually entertaining. This buffoon that thinks America can tell Mexico to pay its bills is running for president! Ha! Well, the joke's on us, America. He has no understanding of the Constitution or the role of the President. On November 29th, the buffoon tweeted, *"Nobody should be allowed to burn the American flag - if they do, there must be consequences or perhaps loss of citizenship or year in jail!"* So much for *Texas vs. Johnson*, the Supreme Court case that guarantees the freedom of speech includes the right to burn the United States flag.

Throughout his campaign, Trump also stated that Hillary Clinton wants to repeal the second amendment. First of all, there is no evidence that it is a true statement. Hillary Clinton literally never said that or anything close to it. She wants the same gun protections most Americans would like, such as people on the no-fly list also be placed on a no-gun buying list; background checks for every gun buyer, no matter how long it takes; and doing away with the so called gun show loop hole. Never once has she said "repeal" or to get rid of the second amendment, or that she would take our guns. Not once. Yet, when Donald Trump repeated this lie, no one called him on it. No one said, "Hey, you know what Donald that is a false statement." Ever. And, on top of that obvious flaw in coverage, no one ever asked him if he thought the President could just go and repeal an amendment. It is quite an undertaking. And he obviously has no idea how it works. Repealing an amendment means making a new amendment to repeal the old amendment. To make an amendment, it takes two-thirds of state legislatures or two-thirds of both the House and the Senate to propose the new amendment. It's not easy. And it does not involve the President. At all. At any stage. So, why the media would not ask him how amendments work or why he thinks the president could unilaterally repeal an amendment may have been a good question for the media to ask Donald Trump.

The President-Elect also seems to think that international law does not apply to him as President of the United States. The media allowed him to run with a crazy waterboarding promise that would get us in trouble internationally and require our soldiers break their oath. They would either have to follow the laws they are bound by internationally or the orders of their Commander in Chief. And no one asked him about it. No one said hey you cannot do that. In a TIME article in May 2016, Chris Edelson reported:

> Trump has also said that he would order the military to carry out torture, declaring that they would follow his orders, whether lawful or not. Trump seemed to later backtrack when he said he would "stay within the laws" in responding to ISIS — but his new position does not immediately make sense.

> Trump said he'd like to change the law to allow waterboarding. But waterboarding is torture. Torture, by definition, is illegal—both under U.S. law and international law. The U.S. has signed a treaty prohibiting torture and other cruel, inhuman, or degrading treatment or punishment. Would Trump have the U.S. withdraw from the treaty? If Congress did not support him, would he act anyway?

Trump has no understanding of international law. The idea that he could change the law to match his wishes to get information from informants is scary. And reporters should have asked him about it every time they interviewed him. They never cared enough about the facts from a person running for the highest position in the world. They just needed ratings.

Let us talk about taxes. Every presidential nominee since Richard Nixon has released their taxes so the people know they are not bound to foreign entities, pay their fair share of taxes to support our infrastructure and military, gives to the charities they claim to have given, and have nothing else financially binding that would compromise their position or the United States' position across the world. It is important. President Nixon was reluctant to release his tax returns because he had donated some papers to the National Archives. He claimed a huge deduction that year and barely paid any taxes at all. When the timing of his gift to the Archives came into question, Nixon famously stated, "I welcome this kind of examination, because people have got to know whether or not their president is a crook. Well, I am not a crook." Turns out, he was a crook. Donald Trump promised to release his tax returns no less than 17 times. Yet he never released them.

Trump has so many different and invalid excuses for not releasing his taxes. He claims he is under audit and it is not allowed. But Nixon released his while under IRS audit. So that excuse falls flat. He claims not much can be gleaned from tax returns anyway, so it is not important. Interestingly, his campaign used Hillary's tax returns to make bogus claims about foreign involvement, so hers were important to them. Why did the media not sift that out? Kellyanne Conway repeatedly answered questions about Donald Trump by pivoting to information revealed by the tax returns from the Clinton Foundation, founded by Hillary and Bill Clinton. So, apparently the other candidate's tax returns were important to his campaign staff. Interesting. His most laughable response was the voters do not care. Democrats begged and pleaded with the media to do its job and ask for his tax returns. Of course, Trump's followers did not care. They believe he has all the answers, even though he could not pass a tenth grade civics exam. If he tells them his taxes are not important, then to them it is not important. He is "Dear Leader" after all.

Unfortunately, another mistake the media made was grossly underestimating the racist underbelly of the Republican Party Trump was ginning up. "The media made a mistake by covering Trump's candidacy at the start as some sort of joke or media prank," notes Danielle S. Allen, a political scientist at Harvard. We never took him seriously. We looked at him as a joke; a laughable caricature that thinks he has a chance at being president someday. Kristoff's article continued to interview political scientists and came up with the same results. Ralph Begleiter, a professor at the University of Delaware noted that dimwitted Sarah Palin was a more serious candidate for Vice President than Trump was for President. Frankly, that is embarrassing. Kristoff noted that Tom Brokaw has asked pointed questions to Trump. Brokaw says that when journalists have indeed questioned Trump's untrue statements, nothing much happens: "His followers find fault with the questions, not with his often incomplete, erroneous or feeble answers." No matter what Donald Trump says, his followers think it is perfect. It is truly bizarre. He says he is getting big banking out of government, and his followers praise his appointments of four former Goldman Sachs employees. These same followers ripped Hillary Clinton for giving a speech at Goldman Sachs and therefore having to do their bidding. Somehow, Clinton giving a speech disqualifies her from the presidency, but Trump actually appointing them to cabinet positions does not. Their cult leader can do no wrong and they cannot see the fallacy in their argument.

William Randolph Hearst once said, "Hitler is certainly an extraordinary man, we estimate him too lightly in America. He has enormous energy, intense enthusiasm, a marvelous facility for dramatic oratory, and great organizing ability. Of course, all these qualities can be misdirected." And misdirected they were. One can only hope the demagogue Americans just elected by virtue of the Electoral College, and certainly not by popularity, does not find us in the same predicament the Germans found themselves in 80 years ago.

## Chapter 7

*The great masses of the people will more easily fall victims to a big lie than to a small one.* – Adolf Hitler

One of the more remarkable aspects I have found when talking to Fox "news" watchers, are the things about America and progressives and conservatism they believe that simply are not factual. The lies spread about Barack Obama during his presidency put the truths reported about Donald Trump to shame. And these lies have been going on for decades. True followers of Limbaugh, Coulter, Fox "news" and Beck really are in the dark when it comes to the events of the last 30-to-40 years. If one actually listens to them talk, one would think that Reagan balanced the budget, gave every American a gun, made government so small you could barely find it in D.C., and threw immigrants out by the thousands. You would also think Obama drove the debt sky high, is a Muslim, ruined our economy, set up government housing for undocumented workers so they could vote, and lost millions and millions of jobs. The opposite is true *in every example listed* and it is just bizarre that Hannity says our economy and jobs outlook are terrible, and people just blindly repeat it.

Let us examine the deficit and debt for starters. I am not an economist, and therefore will take a preliminary look at these, discuss the paradoxes of pundit analysis, and move on to other oddball conservative beliefs. Many and varied are the excuses that the debt soars when a Republican is in office and diminishes when a

Democrat is in office. First of all, many Fox "news" watchers simply do not know that since, and including, Reagan the debt has risen at a higher rate under Republican presidents than under democratic leadership. Reagan raised the debt level 186% under his watch; Clinton was 32%; Bush 43 was 101%; Bush 41 was at 54%; and Obama saw a 68% increase in the debt while he was President. Bush 41 was only a one-term President so he managed to outspend a two-term President in Clinton, and was close to Obama in a recession in half the time. Often the excuse from Republicans to explain this phenomenon is that Congress controls the spending, and Reagan had a democratic house! I can go along with that, but then you have to attribute the awful train wreck of economy that you seem to think Obama made to the republican congress, right? Of course not, they say, THAT is all Obama. So Reagan's missteps were the Congress and Obama's missteps were Obama's. All the great things during Reagan's watch were Reagan's and all the great things during Obama's watch can be attributed to the Republican Congress. Good to know.

The subtitle to a Chris Mooney article on "Alternet" October 20, 2014, states in the subtitle, "Authoritarian people have a stronger emotional need for an outlet like Fox, where they can find affirmation and escape factual challenges to their beliefs." Mooney goes on to explain how badly misinformed Fox "news" watchers are using six events or occurrences that they are badly off base in what they believe and what actually happened. The first is the Iraq war. Sixty-one percent of Fox "news" watchers think we actually found weapons of mass destruction (WMD) in Iraq. No WMD were ever found. Only 14 percent of MSNBC watchers believe we actually found WMD in Iraq. Republicans believe whatever fits their narrative. Thirty percent of Fox watchers believe Obama was not born in the United States, which is more than the combined number for other networks. Fox watchers never research anything because what they are being told fits their narrative, so why look it up. They have their answer. They even believe stories that contradict themselves in order to put Obama or any other progressive in a bad light. For example, they believe Obama is a Muslim from childhood, based on loose familial connections, but that he also attended Jeremiah Wright's controversial Christian church in Chicago. He actually was a member of Wright's church until it came under controversy in 2008 and has since attended a Southern Baptist church in Maryland. There is no evidence whatsoever that he is Muslim. Yet Fox "news" watchers believe it and repeat it.

Fox "news" watchers seem really upset that Barack Obama has the unemployment numbers at 4.6% and dropping as well. Never mind that low unemployment numbers mean that Americans have jobs, and that is usually a good thing. Apparently, the right likes low unemployment unless it is under Obama because he turned the recession around and put America back to work. The excuses on why these numbers, which Obama has absolutely nothing to do with crunching, are like Iraq, many and varied. One is that Obama "changed the formula" and calculates the numbers differently than any other president ever. Again, Obama does not actually sit there and do math and get these results on his own. The United States Bureau of Labor Statistics calculates the unemployment and they always have.. Another false cause Fox "news" and right-wing pundits attribute to Obama's success is that there are so many people leaving the workforce that cannot find jobs and therefore are no longer being counted. According to Donald Trump, in a speech after he won the New Hampshire primary, "The number's probably 28, 29, as high as 35. In fact, I even heard recently 42 percent." And it is, if you count as unemployed all the retired people in America, any student 16 and over that is not working, stay-at-home moms, or anyone who is not working for whatever reason. But that is not how we measure unemployment in this country. The BLS uses 6 methods to calculate the unemployment rate, and the U3 is considered the one that we use as measurement. That's it. No trickery or manipulation by someone that has nothing to do with it – just straight numbers.

Another propaganda tool used by the right-wing pundits is to say that "Christianity is under attack" in America. Somehow, someway Christians think they are going to be beheaded at any moment because of progressives "coddling" religions other than Christians. Again, it is just out there and bizarre, but they repeat these stories as though they are fact. We all heard CNN contributor and Trump advisor Corey Lewandowski say that we could all say "Merry Christians" now, that Christmas is no longer a pejorative. We have always been able to say Merry Christmas. That was never an issue. It was never banned, or made criminal or anything of the sort. Yet, there are conservatives running around applauding that they can say Merry Christmas this year.

Christians also think that because gays can legally marry in the United States, their rights as a Christian are being taken away.

This one is hard to grasp. So, if a heterosexual couple marries in Oklahoma, does that keep someone from being gay in Nebraska? How does one have anything to do with the other? It has been said – if you do not like gay marriage, do not get gay married. As far as I can tell, literally nothing has changed in your Christian church since gays could marry. Nothing. There is some "gay agenda" out there too. It is mystical and fun and as a gay, I have no idea what it is. Being treated like a human? Is that considered an agenda? If a gay human thinks they should be treated like a human? My, oh my.

There are many more conspiracies that the right has cooked up to gin up their base and make the progressive America-hating left look like the bad guy. Climate change is one. There is not enough time in this effort to delve into the denial of climate change. But they do. They rally against Planned Parenthood, yet where there is Planned Parenthood there is less unwanted pregnancy. As a matter of fact, under Obama's watch, teen pregnancy has dropped to its lowest numbers yet. Give people access to resources and look what happens - progress! But, alas, the right wants to "Make America Great Again", implying going back to a better time than now. We shall see. My money is on now.

## Chapter 8

*I think the only difference between me and the other candidates is that I'm more honest and my women are more beautiful.* – Donald Trump

When talking about fake news in the 2016 election and the 20 years of Fox "news" propaganda – and eventually other Web sites and sources - leading up to the election, one would be remiss not to talk about Hillary Rodham Clinton and the fake news levied against her and her husband over the years. Clinton has had an exemplary career that clearly threatens conservatives because they will go to any length to paint her as the bad guy. As this is not a biography, I want to just touch on some highlights from Clinton's life because a full review would take volumes. For the purposes of propaganda, a simple highlight of how she has lived and how it was reported by the right is sufficient. In fact, it is more than sufficient.

Her entire life has been spent advocating for children's and families' rights. During law school she worked as a staff attorney for the Children's Defense Fund. After graduating from Yale University with a law degree, she co-founded Arkansas Advocates for Children and Families, a group that was tied to Children's Defense Fund. She was appointed by President Jimmy Carter to serve on the Legal Services Corporation, and fought Reagan in the early 1980's to keep it funded appropriately. She married Bill and it became obvious they were going to be players in the Democratic Party for a long time, and the right started firing shots immediately.

Bill Clinton's infidelities are widely documented. He is a philanderer; there is no doubt about it. Honestly, it has nothing to do with Hillary. The fact that she fought to keep her family together, a very Christian principle, one would think the right would concur with her, and praise her ability to stay true to her vows. However, their President-Elect and two of his closest advisors are all on their third wives. So much for family values and a vow before God. She did what most wives do that want to stay married to their husbands, even when their husband cheats on them, and that is fight for their future and hope he is telling the truth when he says he is sorry. I do not believe for one second Bill was, but I understand being the wife that hopes so. It is also important to remember that Hillary is a seasoned, gifted attorney. When it comes to legal matters, she always converts to lawyer mode because it is her comfort zone. Fox "news" has continually reminded their viewers of a comment from Hillary to one of Bill's mistresses, Gennifer Flowers. It is reported that Hillary said, "I would crucify her." My, oh my, that sounds awful. She is literally threatening to crucify this woman? However, Fox "news" and their propaganda machine failed to tell you that it is an answer to the question of cross-examining Flowers on the witness stand after Flowers had changed her story several times. She would be toast for even a mediocre attorney, let alone someone with Hillary Clinton's experience and skill.

The Monica Lewinsky story came out while Bill was president. And Hillary was as graceful as you would expect a woman to be when her husband has cheated on her for the umpteenth time, this time in front of the country and the world. She was hurt and angry. Yet she still did not lash out. Shawn Boburg wrote in the *Washington Post* that the White House was very different after the news broke of Bill's affair. "A chill fell over the White House," and other staffers noted Hillary's solemn behaviors inside the White House that clashed with her stoic public persona. George Stephanopoulos wrote, "She had to do what she had always done before: swallow her doubts, and savage his enemies." She did not speak to Bill for some time and it made life in the White House somber and difficult. Hillary mostly blamed herself for Bill's affairs, saying she was not smart enough or sensitive enough or free enough. She also called Lewinsky a "narcissistic looney toon." In my opinion, those are pretty kind words for the woman who has been trying to land your husband. The reality is that any woman struggles to be civil to her husband's mistresses. In a "Today Show" interview with Matt Lauer, Clinton hinted that the propaganda is already in full swing against her husband, and this may be more of the same. Here's an excerpt:

> Lauer: Are you saying, though, that you're no longer -- that this doesn't upset you anymore? You're almost numb to it?
> Clinton: It's not being numb so much as just being very experienced in the unfortunate mean-spirited give-and-take of American politics right now. So having seen so many of these accusations come and go, having seen people profit, you know, like [the Rev.] Jerry Falwell with videos accusing my husband of murder, of drug-running, seeing some of the things that are written and said about him, my attitude is, you

know, we've been there before. We have seen this before. And I am just going to wait patiently until the truth comes out.

She's not lashing out and she's not angry. She seems calm and calculated, not the sinister person attacking these women as the right has reported. All of the language used was consistent with an educated woman whose husband was caught in an affair and nothing more.

Another popular rumor heard more than once from the propaganda machine: the Clintons will murder people who get in their political way. Interesting. I think the body count is at 33 and growing. I am not kidding about this either, and people believe it. The ever-tactful Ann Coulter stated, "If you attack the Clintons publicly, make sure all your friends know that you are not planning suicide." I think it was supposed to be a joke. The Web site Snopes informs us, "'Body count' lists are not a new phenomenon. Lists documenting all the allegedly "suspicious" deaths of persons connected with the assassination of John F. Kennedy have been circulating for decades." Those creating these lists all seem to use the same techniques: create a long list of every dead person who may have ever known the party being accused play word games, like listing the death as "mysterious" and say "autopsies were not allowed" as opposed to "unneeded" and, most importantly, do not let facts and data get in the way. For instance, if the coroner's report reads the person died of a heart attack, tell your readers "supposed heart failure, alone in the hotel, no one knows for sure." The problem is that coroners *do* know. It is their job to know. Also, if the Clintons' murder those who spread rumors or attack them or make their lives difficult, how are Gennifer Flowers, Monica Lewinsky, Ken Starr, Anthony Weiner, Paula Jones, and any other famous Clinton agitators still alive? Too obvious? Best to hit only the nobodies that get on the Clintons' nerves? Good grief, people. As the Web site Snopes continued, "The list was compiled by Linda Thompson, an Indianapolis lawyer who in 1993 quit her year-old general practice to run her American Justice Federation, a for-profit group that promotes pro-gun causes and various conspiracy theories through a shortwave radio program, a computer bulletin board, and sales of its newsletter and videos. Thompson admitted she had "no direct evidence" of Clinton's killing anyone." But hey, who needs evidence?

The main death the fake news proprietors tell is that of Vince Foster, a staffer who committed suicide. A cursory look at the details tells a thinking, cognitive human that something is amiss about the story of murder and cover up. But no, that does not fit the narrative to spread lies about the Clintons. Foster committed suicide in a park in Washington, D.C., the day after calling his doctor about his depression. There were three investigations into his suicide and all of the investigations, including one by special counsel Kenneth Starr – a republican and professional Clinton hunter - that all ruled his death a suicide. The language is important. When the propagandists talk about suicide, they say "ruled a suicide" as if there were other options and this option barely beat out "shot in the head by Chelsea." "Ruled a suicide" means that's what happened in an autopsy. It was not mysterious or sinister. The man suffered from depression, was being harassed by the "Wall Street Journal," and had to fire some people at the White House. Tragically, it ended with him taking his own life, nothing more and nothing less.

All of the fairy tales on the "Clinton body count list" have one thing in common, they are wildly speculative. People creating the lists say things like "the plane exploded" when it simply crashed, or "he was going to reveal information" when he had worked as an intern, or "no one knows what happened" when the coroner's report or accident report is very clear and leaves no room for doubt. On August 24, 2016, Fox Business ran a story in which anchor Cheryl Casone stated that Google was manipulating search results to filter out negative stories about Clinton, including an attempt to hide her fake body count story. So, a Fox News anchor was upset that Google "filtered out" untrue stories about a mythical trail of bodies by the Clintons that they needed people to read about to spread their propaganda. When asking people why they believe something so blatantly false, they say that the Clintons threatened everyone that could possibly report the truth. There is no evidence of this accusation and no one credible has ever come forward and said as much, but the "news" sources float the idea and so it becomes fact. There are entire Web sites devoted to making it seem like the Clintons murdered dozens and dozens of people. The people trying to tie the deaths of people related only peripherally to the Clintons are a who's who of crazy town. Roger Stone is not allowed on most cable news stations because of wild racism; Julian Assange is holed up in an Argentine embassy in London because he is wanted on rape charges in Sweden; and BlazeTV, headed by Glenn Beck, who has championed crazy on the right for decades lead the charge of crazy town accusers. These people are not remotely credible, yet the right repeats their words as though they are Jesus himself.

The Clintons are also accused of some vague grand scheming over a real estate deal that has been dubbed Whitewater. To hear the right tell the story, the Clintons somehow swindled taxpayers and used their political positions to keep their friends Jim and Susan McDougal out of trouble. The truth is that Bill and Hillary were just out of law school and living fairly modestly while Bill was the Attorney General for Arkansas. They had friends that had an idea for a real estate venture and all four invested in a property to be sold as lots for a profit later down the road. It was 1979, and after the purchase, interest rates soared and no one was buying. The Clintons lost somewhere between $37,000 and $70,000 in the deal. They did not earn any money and they did not steal any money. This was all revealed in released tax returns, so we know this. The rest of the accusation is that the Clintons were using their political power to keep the McDougals out of trouble. Both were found guilty of fraud in an unrelated savings and loan venture. So much for a big story of Bill and Hillary swindling people in Arkansas. They made a bad deal and lost money. Their friends were busted for a bad savings and loan (S&L). A lot of people were busted for bad savings and loans in the 1980's. There are volumes about fraudulent S&Ls in the 1980's. Unfortunately for the right, none of them had anything to do with the Clintons. Ken Starr spent eight years and millions of taxpayer dollars only to conclude, "there is no evidence of wrong doing by the Clintons."

Benghazi. Probably the saddest of all the fake Hillary scandals because it involves the loss of patriot lives. Under the watch of each and every Secretary of State we have ever had, embassies have been attacked and lives have been lost. Under George W. Bush, with Colin Powell and Condoleezza Rice as Secretary of State, 13 embassies were attacked and 60 people died. This is not a widely reported number, unfortunately. It is not actually news; it is the world in which we live. Foreign entities attack Americans. Where was the outrage from Republicans? The Clintons were not involved; nothing to see here. The facts surrounding Benghazi are no different than previous attacks, except that Hillary is hated and she apparently killed them on purpose and did not care that they died. This is, of course, according to any person who watches Fox "news." The American embassy in Libya was attacked and four people died, including Ambassador J. Christopher Stevens. In the aftermath of the attack on the embassy in Benghazi, there were conflicting stories of protests and terror attacks and what went wrong. It was awful. Clinton calls it her biggest regret – those lives lost on her watch.

The question of impropriety seems to lie in how the White House and those involved characterized the attack. When something like this happens, the CIA gives those involved "talking points" – words used in public to describe the events without jeopardizing investigations or divulging secrets or agents. The talking point for the Benghazi tragedy was an anti-Muslim video that was posted online that infuriated people. In the immediate aftermath, the

Administration admitted it was a terrorist attack, supposedly fueled by this video. Hillary Clinton, as Secretary of State, likely knew that and alluded to that in an e-mail to her daughter. The Republican congress has put more man hours into investigating Benghazi than into the assassination of JFK and the Watergate scandal combined. That is a vendetta. They had eight separate investigations, desperately trying to pin Hillary down as a criminal. They failed. She's not. Trey Gowdy, this decade's Ken Starr, tried and tried and failed more than once to find any wrong-doing. Everyone did exactly as they were supposed to do. A few soldiers in the area claimed they could have gotten to the Embassy and made a difference. They were wrong. The committee headed by Gowdy found that to be false. They may have been able to fly there, but, at that point, the damage was done. The four Americans were already dead. But that is what the propaganda says. People that fall for propaganda say, "What about the stand-down order? Why did Clinton hold back our troops?" Well, there never was a stand-down order. Gowdy reported that the soldiers that thought they heard a stand-down order were wrong. And, people, the Secretary of State does not give orders to troops. Ever. If their listeners would just think about what they are being told and look the unbelievable up, we may not have "Orange Hitler" as our President-Elect. What happened at the Embassy in Benghazi is a sad chapter in American history, for sure. But as a negative reflection of Hillary Clinton, it falls way short of palpable.

Hillary Clinton was also crucified for using a private e-mail server during her tenure as Secretary of State, therefore being flippant about the security of our nation. It's also widely reported that Colin Powell used private e-mail servers, but never mind that, their last name is not "Clinton". She may have sent classified e-mails through an unsecured line, but the FBI investigated and found nothing even remotely criminal. FBI Director James Comey, much to the dismay of rabid Republicans just waiting for Clinton blood to spill, were completely dismayed when he recommended the Department of Justice not bring charges against Hillary Clinton. He stated that three of the tens of thousands of e-mails they investigated were classified, but they were improperly marked and there was no way for Clinton to know – in other words – not guilty. According to Comey, no "reasonable prosecutor" would pursue charges against Hillary. Well, the right is not reasonable, so they attacked Comey and the FBI for not reporting what they wanted to hear. Rudolph Giuliani, crazed Trump supporter, said that the "evidence of intent" was overwhelming. He left it at that, and his interviewer, Sean Hannity – also a Trump supporter, did not think it relevant to ask what information Giuliani had that no one else on the entire planet knew. He left it at that. Now his audience runs around saying the evidence of intent was overwhelming. Really? What evidence? There is none.

The right has been investigating Hillary Clinton for over 30 years, and they have yet to find her guilty for anything. She is always found innocent, much to the dismay of the craven Trump supporters screaming "Lock her up!" at his rallies. They think she is such a good criminal and she has coroners and attorneys and hit men and all sorts of sinister ways to stay out of jail. There is zero evidence to support any of these claims, but the last thing Fox "news" watchers need or want are facts. She lost the Electoral College in the November 2016 election and oddly, as she will never run for office again, Gowdy closed his e-mail investigation. So much for the moral obligation of pursing a criminal. The GOP readily admitted they were not really investigating Benghazi to find wrong doing, but instead to attack Hillary Clinton. "This may not be politically correct, but I think that there was a big part of this investigation that was designed to go after people and an individual, Hillary Clinton," Rep. Richard Hanna (R-N.Y.) said in an interview on the radio. There was no evidence, only wild theories of trying to connect dots that just have no relation. Yet people believe it. And they believe Hillary Clinton is the absolute devil from whom we were saved. History will prove otherwise.

## Chapter 9

*The broad masses of a population are more amenable to the appeal of rhetoric than to any other force.* – Adolf Hitler

When Hillary Clinton won the nomination for president in the spring of 2016, there were no holds barred for the lies thrown at her by the right. Some were completely unbelievable, yet the right wing repeated the lies, almost verbatim. The propaganda would start from a Donald Trump tweet, or an obscure conspiracy Web site, or even right on Fox "news." And no one takes the time to look it up. Donald Trump has 10 million followers on Twitter, and most of them believe in him like a cult-like figure, and believe and retweet every word he says. So let's estimate that half of all of his followers retweet his nonsense, now in seconds, 15 million eyes read something Trump said that was completely untrue. But there is no research, no pause, just regurgitating propaganda.

For example, the CIA reported on December 11, 2016, that Russians hacked into some U.S. Web sites and manipulated the news to help Donald Trump win. Trump immediately tweeted, *"Unless you catch "hackers" in the act, it is very hard to determine who was doing the hacking. Why wasn't this brought up before election?"* "That's just silly," laughed John Schindler, who worked for 10 years as an analyst at the National Security Agency. "That is just simply false." However, a Trump supporter told me when the Russian hacking was mentioned said, "They don't know that. Unless you catch hacking when it happens you can't tell who did it." A simple

Google search will show actual IT experts reporting things like "laughable" and "not true" and "where did he get that?" But it is now being repeated all over America. This is how propaganda spreads.

One such lie about Hillary Clinton is that she had developed Parkinson's disease, cancer, or maybe even SOMETHING WORSE. This propaganda was designed to make people fear voting for Hillary Clinton, as she was clearly going to die soon. I wish I was kidding. The lie started with Alex Jones on infowars and ballooned from there. Some Republicans said solemnly, "I think Hillary is really sick. She really needs to relax and slow down." It was one of the more insincere statements I heard from the right about Hillary. These same people were hoping to "lock her up" and chanting "Killary for prison." The problem is that it is a total fabrication. She released a report from a doctor that reported no illness while Donald Trump released a fake report showing that he was going to be the healthiest president ever. That's not really what doctors say, but the right repeated it. They even cut video of Hillary laughing and watching balloons fall at the DNC to show her seizures and confusion. It was really remarkable that they were so poorly done and so easily refuted yet people spread the propaganda as if it were gospel.

Rumors about the Clinton Foundation cheating and being a cash cow for her and Bill to pilfer at will were spread constantly. The problem is twofold with this propaganda. First, she released 35 years of tax returns. Neither she nor Bill received any money from their Foundation. They never used it to pay bills or donate to another charity or anything underhanded. The numbers are all set out for the world to see. Saying anything else is pure speculation and there is no evidence. But, of course, the followers of the right do not need actual evidence or proof – that would ruin their whole platform. The second problem with this lie is that the Clinton Foundation is one of the highest rated non-profits in the world. Well, how can that be? They are the worst people on the entire planet, yet their charity is one of the best in the world. In fact, almost 90 percent of the proceeds from their foundation go back into projects. They operate with almost no overhead. It is remarkable. And while there is no proof that Hillary Clinton ever used her Foundation to pay bills or donate to another charity, this is the exactly what it has been proven that Donald Trump did with his foundation, The Donald J. Trump Foundation. He used his charity to pay legal fees several times, was barred from collecting money for his charity in his home state of New York, and used it to illegally donate to a campaign in Florida. Yet most Fox "news" watchers do not even know that. It does not fit their narrative. However, it was easy for the right to spread the lie about Hillary, all the while ignoring the truth about their favored candidate. How convenient.

Most of the propaganda regarding Hillary's sinister financial gains throughout the years comes from the wildly speculative, evidence-free, and widely debunked book Clinton Cash by Peter Schweitzer. The author himself admits the stories do not have evidence and require a bit of imagination. However, most people that quote the book are not actually quoting the book. They are repeating what Hannity and Coulter and Limbaugh are saying. Even the book's author admits the book is not based in fact. Schweitzer said in April 2015 during an interview on CNN that he had no "direct evidence" of the Clinton's financial improprieties, but suggested a pattern could be developed that implicates some wrong doing. Really? It is embarrassing and wrong to spread propaganda like this knowing it is false. The book was discredited by so many outlets, including the author himself, and Republicans still quote it as gospel. These lies and stories and fabrications caused vitriol and hate for a politician like none I have ever seen. And, sadly, a politician, though not perfect, who has spent her entire adult life serving others.

What would a right-wing conspiracy about a person be without adding the ever-so-scary Muslim element? Huma Abedin is a brilliant and loyal assistant to Hillary Clinton and the latest target of Clinton haters. They have tied her to the Muslim Brotherhood, a terrorist organization, through a journal in which she was the editor for years. Abedin's mother started the Journal for Minority Muslim Affairs and continues to edit the publication. Oddly, the academic journal reports on minority Muslim affairs. Of course, that does not fit the narrative. Representative Sean Duffy, a Republican (and former reality television star) from Wisconsin asked, "Why aren't we talking about Huma Abedin and her ties to the Muslim Brotherhood? Why aren't we talking about the fact that she was an editor for a Sharia newspaper?" This was in response to questions regarding truthful stories about Donald Trump during an interview with CNN. Instead of answering the questions about Trump, he floated this propaganda story to get Republicans off the scent of Trump for a while. And it worked. Conservatives still run around saying she's a Saudi asset who has infiltrated the Clinton campaign in hopes of taking over for the Muslims. This story appears to have originated in the "New York Post," a paper that is definitely a propaganda piece for the right. Rupert Murdoch, the owner of Fox "news" is the owner of the New York Post. Murdoch reportedly disallows stories that reflect negatively on China, as he owns some TV stations in China, and does not want to jeopardize any part of his media empire.

The pundits managed to ride the fabricated e-mail story all the way to the White House as well. The fact that the FBI said there was no case to be had in that story and Clinton had, yet again, done nothing wrong or even remotely criminal, was inconsequential. No matter what anyone said about Trump, the pundits came up with a new e-mail horror story. Five days before the election Fox "news" ran the headline: "Sources: High Probability Clinton's Server Hacked." Sounds ominous, right? Readers look at that and say, "we knew she was hacked. No they are reporting she was hacked." Just a few sentences into the article the reader will find, "The source said the server may have been hacked by up to five foreign intelligence agencies. While other sources believe this is probable, evidence has not emerged to confirm this." So, again, we have no evidence, but there is this outside chance that maybe somewhere along the way there is a chance, so yeah, that headline is fine. A more accurate headline may have been, "No Evidence of Hacking Hillary's Server." But that does not fit the narrative, and Fox "news" watchers do not research or look anything up, so this works. Go with it. What an embarrassment.

During Trump's campaign, Hillary was mocked and derided for giving a paid speech to executives who worked at Goldman Sachs. The right-wing pundit's claimed she now had obligations to them and, if elected, she would bow to Wall Street's wishes and destroy the "little guy". She claimed on the campaign trail that she was no friend of big bankers, although her speeches seemed to tell a different tale. Even the right-leaning Wall Street Journal in an October 9, 2016, article claimed this was normal in politics, claiming Hillary's tactic of saying one thing in private and another in public was pretty much par for the course. They continued that it was not alarming at all, that most politicians were guilty of the same behavior, and that the public comments were the ones to which the politician would eventually be held responsible to adhering. Fox "news" host Sean Hannity ran several articles highlighting Clinton's ties to the banking industry, and made it seem so sinister. People worried that her cozy relationship with the banks would alienate the little guy and be more of the same old stuff. Since his election, Donald Trump has named three Goldman Sachs executives to his transition team, and the right is radio silent. No worries - he knows what he is doing … nothing to see here.

Hillary Clinton has been lied about by the right for 30 plus years, regardless of the lack of any evidence to back up the statements. The people the right-wing propaganda arm of the media is targeting do not need evidence. They need to know they are right, and the Clintons are bad, and Trump is good. So anything that fits that narrative is good reporting, no matter the evidence, or lack thereof – the right has their own narrative. Cries that Muslims and

Mexicans are taking my stuff and that Hillary and the Democrats want to give them more of our stuff ... and ruin America. There is not a single shred of evidence that supports any of these narratives, not one. But, quoting John McCain, facts are pesky things. They get in the way of narratives. They get in the way of "we're right and they're wrong." Fox "news" tells its listeners they are "fair and balanced" and there is no need to go anywhere else. *WE* have done the research for you, believe us, so there is no global warming and Clinton murders people and Sharia law is right around the corner and Obama was born in Kenya and . . . the list goes on and on. Lie after lie.

## Conclusion

*The great strength of the totalitarian state is that it forces those who fear it to*
*imitate it.* – Adolf Hitler

I would like to ask Trump voters if they are alarmed that their chosen candidate is also the chosen candidate for Russia, ISIS, and the KKK. Does that not give you pause? If Nazis are having parades and attacking people in the name of Trump and coming out of hiding, where they should be, is that not a sign that your guy may not be the best choice?

I am afraid a minority of Americans were duped and now the majority has to try fend off the second Holocaust. We had the opportunity to elect an imperfect-yet-gifted lifelong servant. And we have instead elected a narcissistic, self-serving liar to lead us. He has already appointed buffoons, racists, neo-Nazis, Goldman Sachs executives, and wildly inappropriate Generals to key positions. General Flynn retweets conspiracy theories continuously and General Mattis is a known islamaphobe. The Department of Defense in the country founded on freedom of religion should not be led by someone who is known to hate an entire religion. Governor Rick Perry is replacing Ernest Moniz as the Energy Secretary. That seems innocuous, however, Moniz holds a Master's degree and a PhD. from Stanford University and is one of the founding members of the Cyprus Institute and has served at the Massachusetts Institute of

Technology as the Cecil and Ida Green Professor of Physics and Engineering Systems, as the Director of the Energy Initiative, and as the Director of the Laboratory for Energy and the Environment. He's a bad ass. His predecessor, Stephen Chu, holds a Doctorate from the University of California, Berkeley and won a Nobel Prize in Physics. Meanwhile, Perry has a degree in Animal Husbandry from Texas A&M. It is alarming that someone so ill-qualified is now going to be in charge of our energy policy, including safe removal of nuclear waste.

However, with the help of propaganda, that is our lot. It is disgraceful and the feeling of helplessness doesn't seem to go away. The election was stolen by fake news. People believed it. And they also believe that Donald Trump is going to save America from this economic boom that President Obama left him and they will fix the lowest jobless rate we have seen since the last democratic president, and that the self-proclaimed King of Debt is going to get America out of debt. It is bizarre. We are walking off a cliff into the unknown with a spastic cry baby that tweets insults and policy and does not take intelligence reviews because he is so smart. He mimics policies and ideas of Hitler and Americans shake it off as if it cannot happen here. I believe it can and will happen here if we are not vigilant. The signs are there, and without knowledge, history repeats itself time and time again.

This man has a cult-like following. People believe and follow what he says and not what he does. He lied 69 percent of the time he spoke in debates, compared to Hillary's 28 percent, yet the right and Donald Trump spun that to make "Crooked" Hillary seem like the liar. And people bought it hook, line, and sinker. Unfortunately, they still do.

The fact that the right had an absolute conniption that Hillary "may have" been hacked by a foreign entity and then say almost nothing to the fact that the election was "tampered with" by Russia is telling. They report only what fits the narratives and they wait for the truth to blow over via distraction and tweet temper tantrums. It is one thing to play coy with renters, debtors in the form of contracted workers, taxpayers, but these are lives. These are Americans' lives and sometimes Trump doesn't win.

We must encourage our friends on the right to research when they repeat really ridiculous stuff, saying to them, hey did you look that up? I would look it up before telling other people that Hillary and Obama share the same demon possession or that Bill Clinton fathered 27 kids. If it does not sound like it could be true, or tightly follows your very own racist narrative, it's a lie. Do not repeat it. And when you hear others repeating lies, ask them to look it up. When they cheer Trump's moronic cabinet positions, ask them why Perry is qualified to lead the nuclear division of the government when his degree is in goats. Ask them if they know for certain Trump is not financially tied to Russia. And if they cannot say, unequivocally, no, they must stand up to him with us.

We, the American people, must realize our future, and we must stand up to any and all hate. This is not the time to say, "Well let's just wait and see" or "I don't think they really mean that." This is the time to act. When the world looks back on 2016 America in 80 years, like we look back 1930's and 1940's Nazi Germany, are people going to write books about us watching? Are they going to write comparisons of us and the Nazis? I hope not, but the only way to make sure is to stop hate when we see it, every time. Do not wait for someone to help the lady who is having her hijab ripped off while perpetrators yell "Trump!" We must not wait for our Muslim friends to be tattooed or sent to internment camps wondering why we didn't say anything. We, the American people, must stop these homegrown Nazis, out to destroy the very things America stands for and against. And I believe we will.

*We have this image now of Hitler almost as a buffoon, but his speeches made people sincerely believe he would lead them back to greatness.* – ROGER MOORHOUSE

*He had that ability to make people stop thinking critically and just emote.*
EGON HANFSTAENGL on Adolf Hitler

Bibliography

Clinton, Bill. *Between Hope and History*, Random House, NY, NY, 1996.

Clinton, Bill. *My Life,* Knopf Publishers, NY, NY, 2004.

Farquhar, Michael. *A Treasury of Decption,* Penguin Books, NY, NY, 2005.

Goldhagen, Daniel Jonah. *Hitler's Willing Executioners, Ordinary Germans and the Holocaust,* Alfred J. Knopf, Inc., NY, NY, 1996.

Hamerow, Theodore S. *Why We Watched,* W. W. Norton and Company, NY,NY, 2008.

Hoyt, Edwin P. *Hitler's War,* Cooper Square Press, NY, NY, 1988.

Nagorski, Andrew. *Hitlerland, American Eyewitnesses to the Nazi Rise to Power.* Simon and Schuster, NY, NY, 2012.

# Notes

## Introduction

1. Holly Yan, Kristina Sgueglia and Kylie Walker, "Make America White Again: Hate Speech and Crimes Post-election." CNN, November 29, 2016, *http://www.cnn.com/2016/11/10/us/post-election-hate-crimes-and-fears-trnd/*

2. Dan Collins, "Congress Says Yes to Iraq Resolution." CBS News, October 3, 2002, *http://www.cbsnews.com/news/congress-says-yes-to-iraq-resolution/*

3. This is widely known, and a brief description can be found at *http://www.history.com/topics/world-war-ii/joseph-goebbels*

4. Robert Costa, Jose A. DelReal and Jenna Johnson. "Trump Shakes up Campaign, Demotes Top Advisor," Washington Post, August 17, 2016, *https://www.washingtonpost.com/news/post-politics/wp/2016/08/17/trump-reshuffles-staff-in-his-own-image/?utm_term=.008b6b45c40c*

5. Michael Van Der Galien. "Interview With Andrew Breitbart," Hot Air, October 8, 2009, *http://hotair.com/greenroom/archives/2009/10/08/interview-with-andrew-breitbart/*

Chapter 1

1. Elahe Izadi, "Obama, Thomas Jefferson, and the Fascinating History of the Founding Fathers Defending Muslim Rights," The Washington Post, February 3, 2016, *https://www.washingtonpost.com/news/the-fix/wp/2015/12/11/how-thomas-jefferson-and-other-founding-fathers-defended-muslim-rights/?utm_term=.cb965bcd71f3*

2. Dan Cassino, "How Fox News Created the War on Christmas" Harvard Business Review, December 9, 2016, *https://hbr.org/2016/12/how-fox-news-created-the-war-on-christmas*

3. Vultee, Fred (October 2009). "JUMP BACK JACK, MOHAMMED'S HERE," *Journalism Studies.* 10 (5): 623–638.

4. Jonathan Martin, Jim Rutenberg and Maggie Haberman, "Donald Trump Appoints Media Firebrand to Run Campaign," The New York Times, August 17, 2016, *http://www.nytimes.com/2016/08/18/us/politics/donald-trump-stephen-bannon-paul-manafort.html?_r=0*

5. David Duke's twitter account.

6. Fairly well known, *but http://www.jewishvirtuallibrary.org/jsource/biography/Soros.html* has a biographical account of Soros that verifies this info.

Chapter 2

1. Reading the transcripts of any one of Trump's rallies in the Primary or the General Election will verify he states this frequently. It's like the war cry for white nationalists that fawn all over him.

2. NPR has a really concise, informative account of Ronald Reagan's immigration policy here:
   *http://www.npr.org/templates/story/story.php?storyId=12830 3672*

3. Clinton, Bill. *My Life,* Knopf Publishers, NY, NY, 2004.

4. Clinton, Bill. *Between Hope and History.* Random House, 1996.

5. Only citizens can register to vote. If one goes to vote, and is not on the voting rolls, they are given a provisional ballot. The provisional ballots are checked against the registered voters and if they are not registered, and a non-citizen would not be, their vote is invalidated.

6. This is from an interview with ABC News' president in May 2003. He likes Fox's slogan but asks O'Reilly if we report, we decide would be more appropriate, and O'Reilly agrees it would.
   http://www.historycommons.org/context.jsp?item=a100796f oxbegins "Context of 'October 7, 1996: Fox News Begins Broadcasting; Provides Conservative Alternative to 'Liberal Bias' of US News Reporting"

7. Coulter's own website, "Bush's America: Roach Motel," June 6, 2007, Http://www.humanevents.com/article.php?id=21029)

8. America with Jorge Ramos, http://mediamatters.org/embed/clips/2015/05/27/40128/fusion-America-20120526-coulter, 26 May 2015.

9. *The Criminalization of Immigration in the United States:* Walter Ewing, Ph.D., Daniel E. Martínez, Ph.D. and Rubén G. Rumbaut, Ph.D. July 13, 2015, American Immigration Council.

10. Hitler's views on race and hatred of Jews is documented well here as are his ideas of pure bloodlines. Http://www.ushmm.org/wlc/en/article.php?moduleId=10007457

11. The Holocaust Museum has a wide variety of sort articles that are useful in learning about The Third Reich. More here: Http://www.ushmm.org/wlc/en/article.php?moduleId=10007819

12. A quick perusal of criminality amongst immigrants shows that most are law abiding. More documentation is here: Http://immigration.procon.org/view.resource.php?resourceID=00844

13. Coulter, Ann. *Adios America*, Regnery Publishing, 2016.

14. It has been widely reported that deportations are not financially feasible. A good break down is here. Drew, Kate. "This Is What Trump's Wall Will Cost",

http://www.cnbc.com/2015/10/09/this-is-what-trumps-border-wall-could-cost-us.html

15. A government study with prisoner recidivism is here. Kaeble,, Danielle and Glaze, Lauren, "Prison Population" Http://www.bjs.gov/content/pub/pdf/rprts05p510.pdf

16. The easiest version of Kathryn Steinle is on wikipedia. You can google her story and get most of the same facts of her death.

Chapter 3

1. DONALD J. TRUMP STATEMENT ON PREVENTING MUSLIM IMMIGRATION. December 7th, 2015, https://www.donaldjtrump.com/press-releases/donald-j.-trump-statement-on-preventing-muslim-immigration.

2. Lean, Nathan, "Fox News' War on Muslims," Salon.com, September 11, 2012, http://www.salon.com/2012/09/11/fox_news_war_on_muslims/

3. Ellen, "Laura Ingraham and Dick Morris Agree: The Purpose of Ground Zero Mosque is to Indoctrinate American Muslims in Revolting Sharia Law," August 26, 2010, http://www.newshounds.us/2010/08/26/laura_ingraham_and_dick_morris_agree_purpose_of_ground_zero_mosque_is_to_indoctrinate_american_muslims_in_revolting_sharia_law_.php

4. Henderson, Alex, "10 Worst Terror Attacks by Extreme Christians and Far Right Men", August 2013, http://www.alternet.org/tea-party-and-right/10-worst-terror-attacks-extreme-christians-and-far-right-white-men

5. Joe Stumpe; Monica Davey (June 1, 2009), "Abortion Doctor Shot to Death in Kansas Church," The New York Times. p. A1. Retrieved January 22, 2013.

6. Ann Coulter's twitter account, November 13, 2015.

7. ""Statistics of the World Jewish Population" http://www.ibiblio.org/yiddish/Book/Cohen/stat.htm

8. Another example of fake news being believed and people acting on the falsehood and vilifying a group of people that never deserved to be maligned. http://www.jewishhistory.org/world-war-i-and-the-jews/

9. Walther, Karine. Assistant Professor of History at the Georgetown University School of Foreign Service in Qatar. Her book, *Sacred Interests: The United States and the Islamic World, 1821-1921* traces the impact of American Islamophobia on American foreign relations in the long nineteenth century. http://www.rawstory.com/2015/11/islamophobia-is-an-american-tradition-that-emerged-long-before-911/

10. Really lame website but shares the really lame ideas that Christians should be converting non-Christians. It is their stated goal. http://www.hcna.us/columns/non-christians.html

11. This was widely reported. In 2011 Beck agreed with Herman Cain, then a hopeful for the Republican nomination. A

breakdown is here:
http://www.huffingtonpost.com/2011/06/14/beck-i-would-be-uncomfort_n_876875.html

12. More from the Holocaust museum archives here:
https://www.ushmm.org/outreach/en/article.php?ModuleId=1
0007695

13. Trump's exact words when asked about registering muslims was, "I would certainly implement that. Absolutely." Hillyard, Vaughn, "Trump's Plan for a Muslim Database Draws Comparison to Nazi Germany," MSNBC, November 19, 2015, http://www.msnbc.com/msnbc/trump-would-certainly-implement-muslim-database

14. More from Herman Cain on muslims holding government positions. Keyes, Scott, "Herman Cain Tells thinkprogress 'I will not' Appoint a Muslim in my Administration," Think Progress, March 26, 2011,
https://thinkprogress.org/exclusive-herman-cain-tells-thinkprogress-i-will-not-appoint-a-muslim-in-my-administration-158c8bead223#.eghjyncke

15. David Futrelle's website, article by him as well. This is a totally left-leaning completely biased site. He does screen shot all of his social media claims, so it is difficult to argue. Upon seeing the screen shots, one could easily go back to the individual tweets or posts to verify David's findings. This particular article is from June 19, 2016. "Bigots Swarm an American Muslim Writer After Daily Caller Attacks Her for Innocuous Tweet."

http://www.wehuntedthemammoth.com/2016/06/19/bigots-swarm-an-american-muslim-writer-after-daily-caller-attacks-her-for-innocuous-tweet/

Chapter 4

1. Bump, Philip, "Donald Trump Reverses Course For The Man Who Attacked Protester. But Could He Do It?" The Washington Post, March 15, 2016, https://www.washingtonpost.com/news/the-fix/wp/2016/03/10/trump-once-said-he-would-pay-legal-fees-for-people-who-beat-up-protesters-now-that-its-happened-can-he/?utm_term=.e2b1730f295f

2. Edkins, Brett, "Study: Trump Benefitted From Overwhelmingly Negative Tone of Election Coverage," Forbes Magazine, December 13, 2016, http://www.forbes.com/sites/brettedkins/2016/12/13/trump-benefited-from-overwhelmingly-negative-tone-of-election-news-coverage-study-finds/#6385ffca6093

3. It is widely known that Donald Trump was the chief antagonist in the "birther" movement, designed to prove Barack Obama was not born in the United States of America. You can check his twitter feed for numerous tweets concerning this and he said it in various forms.

4. Milavonavich, Zoran, PhD, Professor of Sociology and Anthropology. "Freedom of Speech and Freedom of the Press" is one of the articles on Lincoln University's extensive criminal justice website. Lincoln University is located near

Kennett Square in Pennsylvania. www.Lincoln.edu/criminal justice/hr/speech.htm

5. The Holocaust Museum has information on all the "rules" the Third Reich implemented to retard the press. https://www.ushmm.org/wlc/en/article.php?ModuleId=10007 655

6. Begley, Sarah, "Donald Trump Revokes Washington Post Press Credentials," Time Magazine, June 13, 2016, http://time.com/4367449/donald-trump-washington-post-press-credentials/

7. Eversley, Melanie, "Post Election Hate Crime Surge Worse Than Post 9/11, Experts Say," USAToday, November 12, 2016, http://www.usatoday.com/story/news/2016/11/12/post-election-spate-hate-crimes-worse-than-post-911-experts-say/93681294/

8. Ly, Laura, "Muslim NYPD Officer Harassed, Told to Go Back to Her Country", CNN December 6, 2016, http://www.cnn.com/2016/12/05/us/muslim-nypd-officer-harassed-trnd/

9. Holt, Stefan, "Muslim Woman Harassed On Subway By 3 Men Calling Her Terrorist, Chant Trump's Name: NYPD", NBC New York, December 2, 2016, http://www.nbcnewyork.com/news/local/Muslim-Woman-Harassed-Subway-Called-Terrorist-Donald-Trump-Chant-404329066.html

10. Yamamoto, Jane and Lloyd, Christopher "Teacher Accused of Telling Parents They Will Be Deported," NBC Los

Angeles, November 11, 2016,
http://www.nbclosangeles.com/news/local/Teacher-
President-Election-Donald-Trump-Deportation-Immigration-
400851681.html

11. Lang, Cecilia, "Fake News Onslaught Targets Pizzeria As
Nest Of Child Trafficking," The New York Times,
November 21, 2016.
http://www.nytimes.com/2016/11/21/technology/fact-check-
this-pizzeria-is-not-a-child-trafficking-site.html

12. Bowerman, Mary, "Sandy Hook Denier Arrested After Death
Threats Made To Parent of Victim," December 7, 2016,
USAToday. http://www.usatoday.com/story/news/nation-
now/2016/12/07/truther-arrested-after-death-threats-made-
parent-sandy-hook-shooting-vicitm/95085868/

13. As of January 9, 2017, Trump has still not held a press
conference. His last was July 27, 2016.

Chapter 5

1. King, Brittany, "The Unique Outrage of Excusing Racism By
Saying I Have a Black Friend", Elite Daily,  October 28,
2015, http://elitedaily.com/life/culture/excusing-racism-
black-friend/1262977.

2. On the contrary, it is one the tenants of racism to single a few
"good ones" out while vilifying the group. There was an
African American at one of Trump's rallies and he said,
"Look at my African American!" Remember, after Donald
Trump said Mexico was sending over it's worst, the

criminals and the rapists, he finished it up by saying, "some I assume are good people."

3. In a speech in Munich on April 13, 1923, Hitler shouted, " THE WHOLE WORLD OF NATURE IS A MIGHTY STRUGGLE BETWEEN STRENGTH AND WEAKNESS - AN ETERNAL VICTORY OF THE STRONG OVER THE WEAK." A lot of Hitler's speeches are in ALL CAPS, which is weird, but that is how they are transcribed. It seems the parts of Hitler's speeches he emphasized, are now emphasized with capital letters.

4. Hamilton, Marci, "Why Are White, Uneducated Voters Voting For Trump", Newsweek, November 1, 2016, http://www.newsweek.com/why-are-white-uneducated-voters-voting-trump-515368

5. Most people with any interest in Adolf Hitler have seen the creepy photos of him practicing his speeches in front of mirrors. There are some here if you are interested: http://rarehistoricalphotos.com/hitler-rehearsing-speech-front-mirror-1925/

6. Alfred Delp's story can be found here http://www.ignatianspirituality.com/ignatian-voices/20th-century-ignatian-voices/alfred-delp-sj

7. Bernard Lichtenberg's story can be found here http://the-american-catholic.com/2010/02/14/blessed-bernard-lichtenberg-and-courage/

8. The History Place has a fairly exhaustive study of Adolf Hitler the early years here http://www.historyplace.com/worldwar2/riseofhitler/boyhood.htm

9. Benen, Steve, "The Parts of the Carrier Deal Trump Doesn't Want to Talk About," The Maddow Blog on MSNBC, December 1, 2016, http://www.msnbc.com/rachel-maddow-show/the-parts-the-carrier-deal-trump-doesnt-want-talk-about

10. Savransky, Rebecca, "Boeing Responds To Trump: Air Force One Deal is For 170 Million," The Hill, December 6, 2016, http://thehill.com/homenews/campaign/308990-boeing-says-it-is-under-170-million-contract-to-work-on-air-force-one

11. Flores, Reena, "Trump Tweets on Clinton Winning the Popular Vote." CBSNews, December 21, 2016, http://www.cbsnews.com/news/trump-tweets-on-clinton-winning-popular-vote/

12. The transition approval polls have gotten worse for Donald Trump as much as Barack Obama went up during the same time. Information here: Saad, Lydia. "Approval of Trump Transition Still Low As Inauguration Nears," Gallup, January 13, 2017, http://www.gallup.com/poll/201833/approval-trump-transition-low-inauguration-nears.aspx

13. Flores, Reena, "Trump Tweets on Clinton Winning the Popular Vote." CBSNews, December 21, 2016, http://www.cbsnews.com/news/trump-tweets-on-clinton-winning-popular-vote/

14. Seipel, Arnie, "Fact Check: Trump Falsely Claims Landslide Victory," NPR, December 11, 2016, http://www.npr.org/2016/12/11/505182622/fact-check-trump-claims-a-massive-landslide-victory-but-history-differs

15. Paquette, Danielle, "Donald Trump Insulted A Union Leader on Twitter. Then The Phone Started to Ring." The Washington Post, December 7, 2016, https://www.washingtonpost.com/news/wonk/wp/2016/12/07/donald-trump-retaliated-against-a-union-leader-on-twitter-then-his-phone-started-to-ring/?utm_term=.124fa75c8fd7

16. Woods, James, "Happy Veterans Day? 5 Times Republicans in Congress Screwed Veterans," US Uncut, November 11, 2015, http://usuncut.com/politics/happy-veterans-day-5-times-republicans-in-congress-screwed-veterans/

17. Rucker, Philip, "Trump Slams McCain For Being Captured In Vietnam; Other Republicans Quickly Condemn Him," The Washington Post, July 18, 2015, https://www.washingtonpost.com/news/post-politics/wp/2015/07/18/trump-slams-mccain-for-being-captured-in-vietnam/?utm_term=.c401292bf4af

18. Zaru, Deena, "Michele Bachmann: God Raised Up Donald Trump To Be GOP Nominee," CNN, August 31, 2016, http://www.cnn.com/2016/08/31/politics/michele-bachmann-donald-trump-god-raised-up/

**Chapter 6**

1. Berg, Madelaine, "Donald Trump May Hate The Media, But They Are Both Winners In This Election," Forbes, November 10, 2016, http://www.forbes.com/sites/maddieberg/2016/11/10/donald-trump-may-hate-the-media-but-they-won-with-him/#62709514a810

2. Garofalo, Pat, "Tax Returns, Still MIA," November 7, 2016, US News And World Report, http://www.usnews.com/opinion/thomas-jefferson-street/articles/2016-11-07/donald-trumps-tax-returns-are-a-symbol-of-his-lying-2016-campaign

3. Mcafee, Tierney, "Donald Trump Claims All His Accusers Are Lying, I have No Idea Who These Women Are," People Magazine, October 14, 2016, http://people.com/politics/donald-trump-accusers-lying-no-idea-who-women-are/

4. Hillary Clinton wants the same common sense gun control most Americans polled want. She details her plans here: https://www.hillaryclinton.com/issues/gun-violence-prevention/

5. Armus, Teo, "#Showusyourtaxes Here Is Every Time Donald Trump Promised To Show His Tax Returns," The National Memo, June 28, 2016, http://www.nationalmemo.com/showusyourtaxes-heres-every-time-donald-trump-has-said-he-would-release-his-tax-returns/

6. Thorndike, Joseph, "Donald Trump Won't Release His Tax Returns While Under Audit. But Richard Nixon Did," Forbes, April 5, 2016, http://www.forbes.com/sites/taxanalysts/2016/04/05/donald-trump-wont-release-his-tax-returns-while-under-audit-but-richard-nixon-did/#36983872593d

7. Interestingly, his campaign used Hillary's tax returns to make bogus claims about foreign involvement, so hers were important to them.

8. Rupert, Evelyn. "Conway Defends Trump's Business Holdings, Hits Clinton Foundation," The Hill, December 22, 2016, http://thehill.com/homenews/campaign/311605-conway-defends-trumps-business-holdings-hits-clinton-foundation

9. Popper, Nathaniel, de la Merced, Michael J. and Haberman, Maggie, "Goldman Sachs To Extend Its Reach In Trump Administration," New York Times, December 9, 2016, https://www.nytimes.com/2016/12/09/business/dealbook/goldman-sachs-no-2-seen-as-a-top-economic-adviser-to-trump.html?_r=0

**Chapter 7**

1. The debt and deficit are tricky business and an 500 page book could be written that follows every nuance and allows for every aspect that affects the numbers. Here, I am using straight numbers. An analysis can be found here: Kessler,

Glenn, "Does Obama Have The Worst Record On The National Debt", The Washington Post, December 8, 2014, https://www.washingtonpost.com/news/fact-checker/wp/2014/12/08/does-obama-have-the-worst-record-on-any-president-on-the-national-debt/?utm_term=.92b2629c7e54

2. Casino, Dan, "Ignorance, Partisanship Drive False Beliefs About Obama, Iraq," Fairleigh Dickinson University, January 7, http://publicmind.fdu.edu/2015/false/

3. Holan, Angie Drobnic, "Why Do So Many People Think Barack Obama Is a Muslim?" Politifact, August 26, 2010, http://www.politifact.com/truth-o-meter/article/2010/aug/26/why-do-so-many-people-think-obama-muslim/

4. Streiff, "No Christianity Isn't Dying, But It Is Under Attack," Red State, December 26, 2015, http://www.redstate.com/streiff/2015/12/26/christianity-isnt-dying-attack/ Clearly, I am trying to direct the reader to propaganda. You can have a look at what it looks like and sounds like. For example, "Streiff" describes Dr. Jay Michaelson as "a C-list academic." Look up Dr. Michaelson here: https://en.m.wikipedia.org/wiki/Jay_Michaelson. His qualifications and background make him an authority under any circumstance.

5. Tashman, Brian, "Schafly: Gay Marriage Will Ruin Western Civilization," Right Wing Watch, October 15, 2014, http://www.rightwingwatch.org/post/schlafly-gay-marriage-

will-ruin-western-civilization/ Reading anything Phylis Schafly says is mind boggling, but, there it is.

6. Chait, Jonathan, "Why Republicans Are The Only Climate-Science-Denying Society In The World," New York Magazine, September 27, 2015, http://nymag.com/daily/intelligencer/2015/09/whys-gop-only-science-denying-party-on-earth.html

7. Specter, Michael, "Planned Parenthood Means Fewer Abortions", The New Yorker, August 20, 2015, http://www.newyorker.com/news/daily-comment/planned-parenthood-means-fewer-abortions

8. Patton, Eileen and Livingston, Rachel, "Why Is The Teen Birth Rate Falling?" Pew Research Center, April 29, 2016 http://www.pewresearch.org/fact-tank/2016/04/29/why-is-the-teen-birth-rate-falling/

# Chapter 8

1. Hillary's early history can be found here: http://www.firstladies.org/biographies/firstladies.aspx?biography=43

2. Holmes, Steven, "Reality Check: Did Hillary Clinton Attack Bill Clinton's Accusers?" CNN Politics, October 12, 2016,

http://www.cnn.com/2016/10/11/politics/hillary-clinton-donald-trump-bill-clinton-accusers/

3. Just use any search engine and google "Clinton Death List." You get the laundry list of people who have died and how the right erroneously connects them to the Clintons.

4. Snopes does a really nice job of explaining the "death list" phenomenon and why each and every assumption about he Clintons is incorrect. Mikkelson, David, "Clinton Body Bags," Snopes, July 7, 2016, http://www.snopes.com/politics/clintons/bodycount.asp

5. Gold, Hadas, "CNN Says It Will No Longer Have Trump Ally Roger Stone On Air," Politico, February 23, 2016, http://www.politico.com/blogs/on-media/2016/02/cnn-says-it-will-no-longer-have-trump-ally-roger-stone-on-air-219679

6. Zane, Harry, "Swedish Court Upholds Warrant For Wikileaks Founder Julian Assange On Rape Charge," PBS Newshour, September 16, 2016, http://www.pbs.org/newshour/rundown/swedish-court-upholds-warrant-wikileaks-founder-julian-assange-rape-charge/

7. Johnson, Carrie, "Clinton Scandals, A Guide From Whitewater to The Clinton Foundation," NPR, June 21, 2016, http://www.npr.org/2016/06/12/481718785/clinton-scandals-a-guide-from-whitewater-to-the-clinton-foundation

8. Jacobson, Louis, "Prior To Benghazi, There Were 13 Attacks and 60 Deaths Under George W. Bush?", Politifact, May 12, 2014, http://www.politifact.com/truth-o-

meter/statements/2014/may/12/john-garamendi/prior-benghazi-were-there-13-attacks-embassies-and/

9. Karl, Jonathan, "Benghazi talking Points Had Twelve Versions," ABC News, my 10, 2013, http://abcnews.go.com/blogs/politics/2013/05/exclusive-benghazi-talking-points-underwent-12-revisions-scrubbed-of-terror-references/

10. Toombs, Zachary, "Congress Spent more Time Investigating Benghazi Than 9/11", AJC.com, June 28, 2016, http://www.ajc.com/news/national/congress-spent-more-time-investigating-benghazi-than-did/hlWHBsbtLlZz3UoZ5vSK9J/

11. The Secretary of State does not give orders to troops, but he or she "Ensures the protection of the U.S. Government to American citizens, property, and interests in foreign countries" which is why Hillary calls Benghazi her biggest regret. Chozick, Amy, "Hillary Calls Benghazi Her 'Biggest Regret' As Secretary," The New York Times,January 27, 2014, https://www.nytimes.com/2014/01/28/us/politics/clinton-calls-benghazi-attack-her-biggest-regret-as-secretary.html

12. Brander, Eric, "Hillary Clinton's Email Controversy, Explained," CNN, October 28, 2016 , http://www.cnn.com/2015/09/03/politics/hillary-clinton-email-controversy-explained-2016/

13. Desjardens, Lisa, "5 Things You Might Have Missed In The Clinton Email Report", PBS, May 26, 2016,

http://www.pbs.org/newshour/rundown/5-things-you-might-have-missed-in-the-clinton-email-report/

14. Brander, Eric, "Hillary Clinton's Email Controversy, Explained," CNN, October 28, 2016 , http://www.cnn.com/2015/09/03/politics/hillary-clinton-email-controversy-explained-2016/

15. Landler, Mark and Lichtblau, Eric, "FBI Director Comey Recommends No Charges For Hillary Clinton On Email", The New York Times, July 5, 2016, https://www.nytimes.com/2016/07/06/us/politics/hillary-clinton-fbi-email-comey.html

## Chapter 9

1. Hoft, Jim, "Expert Analysis Finds Hillary Clinton's Recent Seizures A Sign of Brain Damage," The Gateway Pundit, August 6, 2016, http://www.thegatewaypundit.com/2016/08/expert-analysis-finds-hillary-clintons-recent-seizures-sign-brain-damage/ (Interesting sidenote: now President Trump has given The Gateway Pundit White House Press Credentials.)

2. Rupert, Evelyn, "Conway Defends Trump's Business Holdings, Hits Clinton Foundation," The Hill, December 16, 2006, http://thehill.com/homenews/campaign/311605-conway-defends-trumps-business-holdings-hits-clinton-foundation

3. Hillary's, dating back to 2001, and Vice President Tim Kaine's taxes are here: https://www.hillaryclinton.com/page/tax-returns/ Bill Clinton's are here: http://www.taxhistory.org/www/website.nsf/web/presidential taxreturns

4. There are several organizations that rate charities, and The Clinton Foundation always ranks high. Here's one: https://www.charitynavigator.org/index.cfm?bay=search.sum mary&orgid=16680 Trump's charity has not had enough activity to rank on any of the ranking sites.

5. Farenthold, David, "Trump used $258,000 From His Charity to Settle Legal Problems", The Washington Post, September 20, 2016, https://www.washingtonpost.com/politics/trump-used-258000-from-his-charity-to-settle-legal-problems/2016/09/20/adc88f9c-7d11-11e6-ac8e-cf8e0dd91dc7_story.html?utm_term=.3362b1fa593f

6. Eder, Steve, "State Attorney General Orders Trump Foundation To Cease Raising Money in New York," The New York Times, October 4, 2016 https://www.nytimes.com/2016/10/04/us/politics/trump-foundation-money.html?_r=0

7. FoxNews staff, "High Chance Clinton's Server Was Breached," FoxNews, November 3, 2016, http://www.foxnews.com/politics/2016/11/03/sources-99-

percent-chance-foreign-intel-agencies-breached-clinton-server.htm

8. Kertscher, Tom, "No Evidence To Back Claim That Huma Abedin Has Ties To Muslim Brotherhood," Politifact, September 14, 2016, http://www.politifact.com/wisconsin/statements/2016/sep/14/sean-duffy/top-hillary-clinton-aide-has-ties-muslim-brotherho/

9. Kahn, Joseph, The New York Times, "Murdoch's Business In China, It's Business and It's Personal," June 26, 2007, http://www.nytimes.com/2007/06/26/world/asia/26murdoch.html

10. Hannity Staff, "Here's A List of the 17 Most Damaging Wikileaks So Far," The Sean Hannity Show, no date, http://m.hannity.com/articles/election-493995/heres-a-list-of-the-17-15208843/

About the author

Kelly Carey lives in Salisbury, Maryland. She earned a
Bachelor of Arts in History from Salisbury University in 2005.
She is considered a political junkie and has
proudly voted three times each for
Hillary Clinton and Barack Obama for
President of the United States of America.

41033920R00092

Made in the USA
Middletown, DE
01 March 2017